Praise for the Most Transformational and Liberating Journey of Healing, Which You're about to Embark on

"I have been through many therapies, but nothing seemed to make me feel enough just as I am."

"Fiona is amazing! I have been through many therapies, but nothing seemed to make me feel enough just as I am. My session with Fiona revealed the real root cause behind my issue – unhappy relationships. It liberated me from loads of guilt, from the feeling that I must have done something wrong, from the loneliness I felt. I was so unready to go on with my life after a sequence of unfortunate events and unhealthy relationships. Now I can start living again, stop fearing rejection, and stop feeling that the good ones are not for me. Somehow, after the session, I felt that I am ready for the new because I know now that these were just my beliefs and we changed them. Just like this. Just as if she used a magic wand. Just stunning. It is a truly transformational therapy."

– Aga, Poland

"Your energy is truly amazing!"

"Fiona, I just want to thank you for our session. It really helped me to understand so much about myself and my past relationship choices. I still listen to my transformational recording most days as your energy is truly amazing! Every time I listen, I get the most infectious belief in myself and I know I am worthy of love and attracting the right life partner. My family and friends have even noticed a difference in me and tell me I am like a beacon radiating love. I can't thank you enough as I finally feel at peace with myself and feel truly happy with or without a relationship."

– Valerie, Poland

"Sceptical by nature, had I not been desperate to escape the pain of a toxic – in fact, abusive – relationship, I might have passed this unique therapy by. I'm so glad I didn't."

"In only two sessions, Fiona got to the root of my self-sabotaging patterns in relationships and gave me a map out of the cycle of pain. Compassionate, wise and gentle, Fiona is the safe pair of hands you need for this process of transformation. I have seen a profound shift: I feel different somehow, stronger in myself and better able to face whatever the future may bring. This is not a magic bullet, and it requires our full participation and commitment, but Fiona is the perfect partner to guide you out of whichever place you feel stuck and on to a path of healing. Thank you, Fiona."

– Deborah, UK

"I cannot recommend Fiona highly enough as a therapist. I am so grateful to you; thank you!"

"I have been plagued with attracting the wrong men into my life, and when I believe a relationship is going well, something always seems to sabotage it. Often I've felt that this is down to me, but for what reasons I have never been entirely sure. It felt like a huge relief to finally understand where these deeply ingrained beliefs and behaviours had come from, and it was a revelation for me to uncover yet more incidences from my childhood that have impacted me throughout my life and in relationships. I now feel empowered by this new knowledge. The transformation part of the session with Fiona made me feel wonderful, and I know now that I am on the path to healing these hurts and making these behaviours and beliefs unfamiliar and obsolete so that I can make better relationship choices. Since my session, I have already begun to notice (particularly about the men in my life) what I will and won't tolerate and accept. I have developed new boundaries and, more importantly, a conscious awareness around my relationships."

– Catherine, UK

"Narcissists were attracted to me like bees to a honey pot! But no more!"

"Fiona, what can I say? You have changed my life. You have changed my relationship with me and my children, and I am no longer the co-dependent person I used to be. I can now completely see why narcissistic men found me as appealing as a honey pot is to a bee, but no more narcissists are getting into this honey's life, thanks to you!"

– Carrie, Ireland

"Fiona is a gifted hypnotherapist and Rapid Transformational Therapy® therapist."

"Fiona is a gifted hypnotherapist and Rapid Transformational Therapy® therapist. I had a session with her about relationships. It was wonderful! As we were preparing, she asked me relevant questions to make sure that she understood my past, as well as what I was hoping to gain from the session. Fiona held space for me as I processed the scenes that came up. She validated my experiences, helping me to break down the meanings and to understand how they all were connected to the way that I look at relationships today. I was made a motivational recording to listen to. She gave me some great advice after the session too. I would highly recommend working with Fiona to anybody interested in exploring their subconscious mind! Thanks again, Fiona."

– Amber, USA

"One thing, in particular, you taught me has changed my life so much and will stay with me forever!"

"I can't thank you enough, Fiona! I gained so much from our session, but one thing, in particular, you taught me has changed my life so much and will stay with me forever. I can still hear your lovely Irish voice saying, 'It's not your relationship-picker button that was broken; it's your relationship-rejector button that was broken.' I wish I had discovered you 20 years ago! Thank you again, Fiona, and keep changing lives!"

– Alison, Wales

"I believed that, to get the love, I had to give and give and do everything relationships."

"I couldn't understand why I kept being in relationships where I would give and give, but I never seemed to get the same back from my partners. Eventually, I would get to the point where I would resent them so much, and in most cases, the relationship would then end. It was only after my session with Fiona that it became so clear that I had a destructive belief that I had been holding on to since childhood, which was to get the love, you have to do everything for everyone else. This made perfect sense, as growing up, my parents were always busy working and looking after my sister who was ill as a child, and the only time I got love and praise was when I was helping around the home to make things easier on my parents. Knowing where this belief came from and changing it for a more empowering belief means I finally talk about my needs and what is important for me in relationships. I still give, but only when there is even give and take and both people's needs are taken into consideration. Thank you for empowering me, Fiona!"

– Luisa, UK

Eat, Pray, Self-love

BREAK FREE FROM DESTRUCTIVE RELATIONSHIP PATTERNS THAT ARE KEEPING YOU STUCK, COME HOME TO SELF AND STEP INTO THE HEALTHY, HAPPY & LOVING RELATIONSHIPS YOU DESERVE

FIONA CHALLIS

Dedication

For my son Jamie. You taught me how to love unconditionally, and you fill my heart with such pride and happiness as I watch you grow into the beautiful, caring and kind man that you're becoming.
Love you xx

Contents

THE H.A.P.P.I.N.E.S.S CODE™ - 35

Throughout the book you'll be guided to additional resources,
when relevant, here is the link
www.rapidrelationshiptherapy.com/bookresources

INTRODUCTION

- What's wrong with me?
- Why do I keep seeing the same destructive patterns in my relationships?
- Why can't I just be in healthy and happy relationships where I am valued, loved and respected?

These are the questions I and most of the women I work with consistently ask after yet another relationship ends or when they get that niggling inner feeling that something isn't quite right in their current relationship.

In the last 20 years, I've asked myself these questions more times than I'd care to remember; however, the last time I did, it felt even more crushing than ever before as I loved him so deeply and I honestly thought he was the one! I believed this was the relationship that would make all the pain of divorce and the years of always attracting the wrong guys and getting hurt worthwhile, as that had led me to him. I thought it was destiny that we met. I mean, we were two Irish people who met in a crowded bar in the middle of Paris, we were both business owners and we both worked in the same industry! What are the chances of that? Was the universe finally listening to me?

Within weeks, we'd fallen head over heels in love; within months, we'd moved in together; and within the first year, we were planning our wedding. Our relationship was moving at lightning speed. But you know when you see two people together and you can just see that they were destined to be together, almost made for each other? That was us. We had the most amazing connection, he felt so familiar and it felt that I'd known him for years. Our friends, family and kids were over the moon to see us so happy together.

His birthday was coming up, and I remember him telling me he'd never really had any birthday parties growing up or in his previous marriage, so I went all out and organised a string of parties, BBQs and lunches over his birthday weekend – I wanted to make this his best birthday yet. I'm no Mary Berry, but I even learned how to bake so I could help his two little daughters make the most spectacular birthday cake for him.

On the evening of the last party, after everyone had left, we sat at the kitchen table, having a glass of wine and reminiscing over the fantastic weekend we'd experienced. I'd never felt so happy, so content and so secure in a relationship, so that evening, I decided to change my Facebook status to 'In a relationship'. Before meeting him, I'd been single for over two years, so that feeling of changing my status was so validating! It was almost like I was screaming to every person I knew, "See, there's nothing wrong with me after all, as I'm in a happy and truly loving relationship!"

But how wrong I was. That very same night, the man I'd fallen so deeply in love with dropped his mask, and I barely recognised the man who was sitting in front of me.

I knew I should just have ended the relationship there and then, but I felt full of shame that I'd yet again managed to attract the wrong guy. I didn't want my friends' and family's pity, with them saying, "Poor Fi. She's so unlucky in love," or "Don't worry, there are plenty more fish in the sea," when mine was more like shark-infested waters! So, I stayed and hoped that, in time, he'd change back into the man I fell in love with – but he didn't. Instead, he threatened to commit suicide if I left him. When I did attempt to leave on one occasion, he sent me a text with his password to his laptop, on which he said he'd written a goodbye letter to his daughters, and he requested I read it to them when he was gone; he knew kids were my weakest link. He then promised he'd get therapy and help, but that was replaced by grand gestures and presents to prove how much he loved me.

Two months later, I had my annual holiday where I rent a villa with a group of my friends and family, and as we'd previously arranged, he joined us. I could see he was drinking too much again, and day by day, his mask slowly started to drop again, but I had my son and his friends there this time, and there was no way in hell that I was putting them at risk. So, after he threw a set of keys at me, which hit me, I finally came to my senses, gathered every bit of courage in my body and mind, and I threw him out of the villa. Go me!

As always, I put on a brave face and carried on regardless, but inside, I was heartbroken. I can honestly say the pain I felt was worse than naturally giving birth to my son, only this pain was invisible.

In the following months, I felt that my life was like a game of snakes and ladders: one day, I'd be in survival mode and just getting on with life, and then I'd sink down into utter exhaustion and struggle to get out bed. I went from feeling pity for myself to anger at him, from shock down to sadness, from sadness back up to anger, and then back down to denial.

Does that sound familiar?

So there I was – single again, deeply unhappy and feeling like my life was falling apart – but this time, instead of rushing into another relationship to avoid the pain, I decided to use the pain as a catalyst to transform my life and relationships because, quite frankly, I'd had enough and I never wanted to feel like that ever again!

Shortly afterwards, I started on a journey of healing and self-discovery so I could finally figure out why I kept attracting the wrong guys and why, no matter how much I put into relationships, the same destructive patterns kept appearing. I needed answers, as I just couldn't understand how everything else in my life – my career, my family and my friendships – was going so well, but when it came to romantic relationships, everything always seemed to go wrong, and I needed to break this vicious cycle I seemed to be stuck in, as the last thing I wanted was for my son to get stuck in the same cycle.

The first part of my journey started with great intentions. I began by doing an inventory of my relationships, trying to find clues or a pattern I could then break. It was like being 16 again and writing a list of the boys I'd kissed so far, only this list didn't feel so great!

I found this first stage of my journey incredibly difficult. As I relived each relationship, I felt a deep shame take over me, as looking back, there were red flags and warning signs right from the very start in most of my relationships, but I chose to ignore them, believing I could change my partners. Sitting with the pain of being cheated on, lied to and used, and being foolish enough to let emotionally unavailable, broken and toxic men into my life time and time again, filled me a sense of unworthiness that went right to the very core of me. It was the type of unworthiness I think only women who've been through similar heart-breaking relationships can understand My self-esteem and self-worth were on the floor, and every day I felt myself sinking deeper and deeper into a black hole that I couldn't see a way out of.

Eat

I felt so empty and had more questions than answers at this stage: Was it me? Was it because I'm unlovable? Was it because I'm not enough? Or was it that I simply wasn't as worthy of love as other women? Feeling overwhelmed, ashamed, empty and incredibly lonely, I turned to my good old friend comfort eating, which somehow made me feel full again. But afterwards, I'd feel so guilty about what I'd eaten – and I didn't want to feel that either – so I turned to my new best friend, rosé wine, to numb the feelings. Then I didn't have to feel any of it!

Unfortunately for me, I wasn't one of those women who got the perfect post-break-up Barbie body. Instead, gallons of wine later with some perimenopausal hormones thrown into the mix, I put on two stone and got the Peppa Pig post-break-up body. I felt like shit, and by then, I also looked like shit! I mean, really, could my life actually get any worse? This journey I'd started on wasn't feeling as good as I thought it would, but I made a 'commit, don't quit' promise to myself to keep going until I got the answers I needed to ensure I could prevent my son getting stuck in the same cycle, so I took a new path.

Pray

So here I was, on the second part of my journey, which consisted of searching the bookshelves of every shop, praying I'd find the book with all the answers. Surely there must be other women out there like me? But there wasn't one book: there were thousands of books, all talking about lots of different reasons why this could be happening to me. My bookshelves were beginning to look like a self-development shop, and I was running out of room, so I then turned to podcasts and YouTube, and I followed every relationship guru I could find. Oddly, a lot of them were men telling women how to have better relationships with men, but there weren't a lot of women advising women, which I found very peculiar.

Despite feeling like I was doing a lot, I still seemed to be getting nowhere fast and I felt I was still stuck in a black hole that I needed to get out of quickly, so I decided to get myself out to talk to other women and I prayed they would have the answers. I joined Facebook groups, I went to seminar after seminar and I registered for every masterclass I could find. Instead of being a food junkie, I'd now become a seminar junkie. However, they served a useful purpose for me, as I finally felt I wasn't the only woman this was happening to, and – unlike when talking to family or friends, where I felt they just didn't understand – I felt I could share openly how

I was feeling with these women, without being judged, criticised or shamed, and I discovered a ton of information about narcissists and co-dependency, neither of which I'd previously heard of. I loved this part of my journey, and I felt incredibly validated, like I was finally being seen and heard by a wonderful community of inspiring women. However, I wanted more than validation: I wanted to heal and to break the cycle so I could finally be happy and be an example to my son. As a result, I set out on the third part of my journey.

At this stage, I was desperate as my search for answers meant I wasn't spending as much time in my business, so it started to suffer, and my health was already being impacted, so I was willing to try anything. I'd heard about the benefits of plant medicine and how it can cleanse you from your past, help you heal, and provide a truly uplifting and enlightening experience, and I thought, *That's what I need! If I can heal and get enlightenment, I'll get the answers I need.*

So, I booked myself into a plant-medicine ceremony in London and had what's called 'kambo', which is the name given to the secretion of a giant monkey frog that lives in the Amazon rainforest. In the ceremony, the kambo treatment was administered by an instructor, who made a small, superficial burn on my upper arm with a red-hot incense stick so the very top layer of the skin was removed, exposing the dermis underneath, and then the kambo secretion was applied to the wound. It didn't hurt, and I didn't think about it that much as there was a lot of chanting and beautiful, relaxing music playing in the background that distracted me. Shortly after having the treatment, I could feel my face swelling up like a frog's face, my body started to overheat, and then, to get rid of the poison, I started to purge (that is, throw my guts up). The instructor told me this was a good thing, as it would get rid of any negativity and toxins in my body, and afterwards, I would feel cleansed and enlightened. Yes, I'd finally lost the plot!

Throwing my guts up in front of 30-odd people is an experience I'll never forget and won't be rushing to do again, but one thing did stick with me from this crazy plant-medicine experience: the words I heard my inner voice say repeatedly during the ceremony, which were these: *Just trust, let go and look within.*

So I did, and this took me on the most amazing journey of self-love and serendipity.

Self-love

I was ready to look within myself and do the inner work, and I made a commitment to myself that I'd dedicate this time to putting myself first so I could heal, and as I did, the right teachers, therapists and coaches seemed to appear in my life just at the right time, with each of them guiding me to look within and complete another piece of the inner work I needed to do. Every step of doing this inner work felt like a light bulb was being lit inside me, giving me the answers I was so desperately seeking and clearing the path ahead for me. Suddenly, everything seemed to make perfect sense, and I finally understood I wasn't broken and there was nothing wrong with me. I felt more connected to myself than ever before, as if I were coming back to myself again, and I felt alive and in love with life. Every step of this part of my journey felt like another piece of my puzzle, and as the puzzle came together, my previous deep senses of loneliness and shame were replaced by a deep inner peace and happiness that I've honestly never experienced or felt before in my life.

My journey – which I now call 'eat, pray, self-love' to represent the different stages of my journey – has completely transformed my relationships and my entire life, and I can honestly say I've never felt so happy.

I reflected on my journey and realised just how much each step I'd taken had transformed my life and my relationships. The first thing I thought about was how incredibly useful it would have been when I was *praying* my way through bookshops, searching for the answers, if I'd found one book to guide me step by step through the inner work needed to get me back to myself. It would have saved a lot of time and money. I then thought, *Why isn't this taught in schools?* I mean, imagine the difference it could make today if children were taught at a much earlier age how to have healthy and happy relationships, regardless of their upbringing or childhood. This is what inspired me to write this book, in which I provide women with a step-by-step guide to learn how to heal, to let go, to let love in, and to have the healthy, happy and loving relationships they deserve.

As I started to plan this book and what to include in it, I looked back at each of the steps that had impacted me profoundly, and when I did, I was completely blown away! I was blown away because, when I put the steps in the order I'd taken them and I looked at the first letter of each step, I recognised that these first letters of the steps on my journey together spell 'happiness'.

Let's take a look at the first letter of each of the steps:

H – Heal from the wounds of your past

A – Attachment styles

P – Programming and patterns

P – Protector parts

I – Inner child

N – Nervous-system regulation

E – Embodied & somatic healing

S – Secure self

S – Self-love

Was this serendipity? Had I finally cracked the code to **happiness** and to having happy relationships? Or was this perhaps my enlightenment from my plant-medicine experience?

I was so inspired when I saw this, and it just confirmed that my decision to write this book had been the right one and that I had to share these nine steps with as many women as possible, as taking these nine steps could – like they did for me – take them from a place of self-abandonment to one of self-love and from a place of hurt to a place of happiness, and so **The H.A.P.P.I.N.E.S.S Code™**, my nine-step program towards happiness, was born, and the contents of this book I was planning unfolded naturally.

Happiness and love are our birthright, but unlike the fairy tales that many of us grew up with and the happy endings you see in romance books – such as the wonderfully written and original *Eat Pray Love* by Elizabeth Gilbert,[1] and the movie based on it,[2] in which Julia Roberts sails off into the sunset in Bali to spend her life with a hot, gorgeous, sexy, incredibly sensitive and charming lover – in real life, to find the true, authentic love and happiness that you deserve there is an extra stage in the journey, so it becomes this:

- Eat
- Pray
- **Self-love**
- Love

Having self-love is the key to having healthy, and happy relationships as the relationship we have with self shapes all other relationships in our life.

In the following pages, I'm going to guide you through each of the nine steps I took on my own journey that was leading me towards **happiness**, which are the steps you need to take in the self-love stage. When you master self-love, you'll then have a blueprint for giving and receiving love and for having healthy, happy and loving relationships. I'll also be sharing the healing techniques and models from the various modalities that I found the most impactful on my own healing, including Rapid Transformational Therapy® (RTT), hypnosis, neuro-linguistic programming (NLP), positive psychology and somatic healing, to name but a few.

By sharing my story with you and by guiding you through the nine steps, I hope it will help you to accelerate your own healing without having to go through crazy plant-medicine experiences looking for answers and without having to spend years in therapy.

Who'd have thought that so much hurt could lead to so much happiness?

Initially, I set out on this journey to heal myself; however, on seeing the impact my healing has had not just on my own life but also on those around me, I became completely compelled to help other women on a similar journey, and I became incredibly passionate about teaching these nine steps towards happiness to the younger generation, such as my son. Fast forward to today, and after retraining as a relationship therapist, somatic-healing coach and positive-psychology coach, I now run a successful therapy and coaching practice, and my plans to bring **The H.A.P.P.I.N.E.S.S Code**™ into the UK school system are well underway.

Wherever you are on your journey today – whether you're just starting out, whether you've already tried loads and still feel stuck, whether you're single and want to attract a healthy relationship, whether you're just coming out of a relationship and are struggling to cope with heartbreak, or whether you're in a relationship but you want avoid patterns repeating themselves and have a happy, healthy relationship – you're in the right place, as this book will guide you step by step on what will be a truly healing, enlightening, transformational journey of self-discovery, in which all the pieces come together like a jigsaw puzzle of your life. When you see the picture the puzzle makes, everything will just make sense, and it's then that you'll be able to heal and break free from your past, rewrite your story and your relationship blueprint, and have the love and happiness you deserve. Who knows what profound impact your healing will have on those around you and where it will take you?

Before we start

I feel so honoured and excited to be your guide on this, but I wouldn't be a very good guide if I didn't warn you about some of the bumps you might hit along the way, so before we get started, let me introduce you to 'the bumps' – otherwise known as the Rules of the Mind, which my mentor and the founder of RTT, Marissa Peer, very kindly taught me – as being aware of these rules at the beginning will be crucial for you to complete this journey successfully.

- **Rule 1** – Your mind's only job is to keep you safe and away from pain.
- **Rule 2** – Your mind's always going to pull you towards the familiar and away from the unfamiliar.
- **Rule 3** – Your mind responds to two things: the words you tell it and the pictures you paint it.

So why are these rules so crucial to your transformation?

Throughout this journey, you're going to be unlearning and relearning, and you're going to be breaking free from old beliefs, patterns and habits that have been keeping you stuck – many of which you may not even realise you've formed over the years. When you do break free of these, your mind is going to do its job of keeping you safe in those old familiar beliefs, patterns and habits that have been keeping you stuck, so you need to be prepared for a bit of push and pull in your mind.

This may sound and feel like this:

- I want to heal, but I can't.
- I want to change, but it's not safe.
- I want to heal, but it's too hard.
- It's safer to stay stuck.
- I just want to quit, as the vicious cycle runs in my family, and I can't change it.

- I've tried some of this before, and it didn't work for me, so I won't try again.

These words you say to yourself and the pictures you paint will further reinforce the message to your mind that it's not safe to heal; this means it's crucial to use positive words and pictures at every stage on this journey, so we can show and tell your wonderful subconscious mind and nervous system that it's safe to heal and be happy.

To ensure we do this, I'll be sharing practical exercises, tools and techniques in this book so that, step by step, we can reprogram your subconscious mind and nervous system as we go, in such a way that it works with us and feels safe. That being the case, I'd really encourage you to complete these exercises in every step, as they're designed to ensure you stick with what will be a truly life-changing journey, and they're designed to make sure that you win, not your mind.

I'd also like to invite you to make a promise to yourself at this stage. I was taught this promise, which Niyc Pidgeon – my mentor and the founder of Positive Psychology Coaching – calls the 'commit, don't quit' promise. This promise helped me immensely on my journey, especially when doing the inner work got hard. On days when I was having a wobble, and my mind was trying to throw me off track and get me to quit, I just kept reminding myself of my promise and why I was doing the work, so I urge you to do the same as making this promise to yourself will keep you on track to complete your transformation. Before we get going on *Step 1*, let's start by writing your promise using the space on the next page.

Please note: Anything that's written within square brackets is an instruction or prompt to help you. You'll see these throughout the book. Any bulleted list that has a heart beside each item is for you to circle one or more of the suggestions or statements.

[Copy the italicised text, adding your feelings as prompted in the space provided on the other page.] *Today, I'm making a 'commit, don't quit' promise that I'll stick to whilst reading this book; I'll complete the exercises provided, so I can get the answers I need, and I'll complete each step.*

I'm committed to my journey, and no matter how hard it gets when doing the inner work, I'll remind myself that I'm making this promise to myself, for myself.

This is so I can be... [write down how you'd like to feel after doing the work and why it's important to you.]

I'm also making this 'commit, don't quit' promise for... [write down who else will benefit from your healing and what the ripple effect will be on those around you.]

Signed,

[sign your name]

Write your promise here

Signed ....

When you have a wobble, which you may have at some points in the journey – please come back to this page and just remind yourself whom you're doing this for and that, by healing yourself, you'll have a profound impact on your life and those around you.

Throughout this book, I'll be getting you to think about the relationships you've had with your parents/caregivers and your previous or current partners; however, please do see this as a book of healing, rather than a book of blame.

Now you know what the journey is going to look like and you're committed to completing it, all you need to do is put your big-girl pants on and get started, so you can heal, you can be happy, and you can have the healthy loving relationships you deserve with yourself and others.

Let's go!

With love,

Fi xx

PS Please be aware that this book is generally aimed at my primary client base in my therapy practice, who are women in romantic relationships with men, and this book has been written from that perspective. However, this doesn't necessarily mean that, if you're of a different gender or in a different kind of relationship, you won't still get something out of this book.

THE
H.A.P.P.I.N.E.S.S
CODE™

H A P P I N E S S

"The process of change requires unlearning. It requires breaking free from the old beliefs, patterns and habits of the old self that are keeping you stuck and reinventing a new loving and empowering self."

– Joe Dispenza

Step 1
Heal Your Past Wounds

As a relationship therapist and positive-psychology coach, I'm fascinated with how people relate and interact with each other. The relationships I find the most fascinating are the relationships each newborn baby has with themself and those around them. When they arrive on this planet, they're the most important person in their tiny little world. They each prioritise the relationship they have with themself; they're so connected with themself, and their needs are top priority. They cry when they're hungry and they scream when they need a nappy change; they don't pretend to like things if they don't, and if their needs aren't being met, they soon let their parents know they aren't happy, even if it's in the middle of the night or first thing in the morning. They laugh, they play and they never try to mould themselves into someone they aren't, just to please others.

But slowly, over time as they grow up, you see those same babies starting to ignore their own needs and putting the needs of others first; instead of naturally expecting love, they learn that, to get love, you must give yourself away, and they prioritise others over themselves. As humans, we're relational beings, we're wired to gain love and connection and to avoid rejection, and we're social creatures who want to fit in and belong, so I can completely understand why these same babies crave that love and belonging, and they're each willing to become a different version of themself in order to get it. But here's the thing: in a healthy, loving and happy relationship and family, you never need to lose yourself, change yourself or mould yourself to be someone you aren't, as your caregivers accept and love you just as you are, and they'll be there to meet your needs and ensure you feel safe.

The unfortunate truth, however, is that very few of the women I work with, myself included, come from an environment like this; instead, some come from families where their physical needs were met, but their emotional needs weren't, and many come from dysfunctional families where – to survive, to get love and to feel like they belong – they had to adapt and to mould themselves into a new role that would help them to establish a place in their family unit and would aid them to get and maintain the love they naturally crave.

In my own childhood, when I was growing up, I remember I couldn't wait to watch the next episode of an American TV drama series called *The Waltons*, which followed the lives of John and Olivia Walton, their seven children (John-Boy, Jason, Mary Ellen,

Erin, Esther, Benjamin, James and Elizabeth), and Grandpa Zeb and Grandma Esther throughout the depression and World War II. They lived in rural Virginia in a beautiful, big, white house with a white picket fence and with a rocking chair on the porch. They were a large and very close-knit family, and despite all the children being so different to one another, they were all celebrated for their uniqueness, and everyone was loved, seen and heard. Every episode was filled with yet another heart-warming story, which resonated with so many children growing up in the late 1970s and early 1980s.

I used to watch it and wish that my family could be more like the Waltons. After all, we were so similar as I also had a father called John and was one of seven children – six girls and one boy – and my grandfather and grandma were integral parts of our family growing up in rural Ireland. Despite it being a TV show, it was based on real people and the real experiences of one family, but the experience in my family couldn't have been more different.

Instead of love, laughter and togetherness, our family grew up in fear. With an alcoholic father who would frequently physically and mentally abuse our mother in front of us, we never quite knew what to expect from one day to the next. The only constant we knew was that children were to be seen and not heard, and we should keep quiet, be good and stay out of his way.

My mother was constantly living in survival mode, and our family was filled with real-life drama and incessant chaos. My eldest sister would be screaming and looking after my mum when things got out of hand, so I always felt it was my job as the second eldest to try to calm my dad down, and if that didn't work, I'd run to the red phone box at the bottom of the housing estate we lived on to call my grandfather or I'd run to get my auntie who lived nearby, as I knew my father would stop when they came into the house, and we'd then be taken to my grandma's house where we'd be safe.

I lost count of how many times my mother said we weren't going back, but we always did, until I was aged 13, when my father appeared suddenly at my school one day to tell me he was leaving and going to England. Despite knowing it was best for him to leave our family, I remember feeling incredibly abandoned.

Afterwards, my mum managed as best she could, but as a single parent, she needed to work a lot to be able to feed and clothe seven children. This meant that she very often wasn't physically or emotionally available for us growing up, so to survive as a family, we all had to do our part and take on the role we needed to play to look after each other. For me, this translated into me taking on the role of fixing everything for everybody.

I remember my therapist asking me, in my very first therapy session, to tell her a little about my childhood and family dynamics. To this I replied, "I can't remember that much of my childhood, but from what I do remember, it wasn't that bad, and I guess it was the same as many growing up in a large Irish family." It was only later that I began to understand how much I'd normalised dysfunctional relationships.

Fast forward to my future relationships, and the same patterns appeared. I was attracting dysfunctional and toxic relationships, including ones with emotionally unavailable or broken men, whom I then tried to fix. I was always giving and sacrificing myself and my own needs to look after and give to others first, as that was the only role I'd ever known, and I'd become so conditioned to thinking, *This is how you get love and connection.*

I hadn't realised this is only how you get love and connection in unhealthy relationships, but in healthy and happy relationships, you never have to sacrifice yourself or your needs, and you don't need to play a role. Instead, you're accepted for being you – all of you, the authentic you. This is something I'd never experienced in relationships until now.

Until I did this inner work, I hadn't really considered how my childhood was impacting my relationship choices. In fact, I'd never really taken the time to consider how my childhood was affecting me, but when I did, I finally began to understand the patterns I've seen in my relationships time and time again: my fear of abandonment, tolerating partners who were emotionally unavailable, accepting breadcrumbs of love, trying to fix and rescue partners, and attracting men who were just like my father, hoping they'd be the one to heal all my wounds from the past. But they didn't; they just reopened them.

Your relationships, both past and present, hold the key to you healing and identifying your unhealed wounds, as it's when you're in relationships that these wounds reveal themselves. These wounds are the reason why you may be attracting emotionally unavailable men, broken men or toxic relationships that are emotionally unsafe for you. They're the reason why so many women people-please, over-give, fix, stay longer than they should, accept unloving behaviour, and/or abandon themselves and their own needs in relationships.

These wounds keep us running on our past conditioning, and they've become so ingrained in us that we aren't even aware of them until we take the time to become consciously aware of them. However, therein lies the problem, as to become consciously aware of our wounds, we must face our pain and hurt head on. This can be a tough process, especially if you try to do it alone, as your wonderful mind is wired to keep you away from pain and will inevitably pull you back into your old familiar patterns, which may include these: running straight into another relationship because being alone is so painful; numbing yourself with food, alcohol or overworking to avoid the pain, which is what I did; or staying in blame or victim mode, as the pain of being here is less than facing it. The problem with this approach is that the pain never goes away because you just carry the same wounds or baggage from one relationship to the next, you still see the same patterns appear, and you effectively keep attracting the same man, just in a different body, meaning you stay stuck in the patterns of attracting and accepting unhealthy relationships.

Revisiting your past relationships and childhood

In this step, I'm going to ask you to trust me as your guide and to take the pain of revisiting your past relationships and childhood as an invitation to heal, an invitation to get unstuck, and an invitation to look inside, do the inner work and ask yourself those tough questions, as that's where you'll have all the answers you're searching for.

It's very important, however, when you do this exercise that you only revisit and don't relive any childhood experiences; this is because, for some reading this book, those experiences could be traumatic. Instead, when answering these questions or completing the following sentences, I'd like you to imagine seeing the answer on a TV screen in your mind's eye and to trust your instinct and the first answer that comes up.

So, when you're ready, let's start to unpack your past:

How would you describe your childhood?

....

....

....

Finish this sentence: My relationship with my caregivers up until the age of nine was...

....

....

....

Finish this sentence: My role model for love and healthy relationships growing up was...

....

....

....

Common childhood learned behaviours

As children, we're wired to seek connection and avoid rejection. We want to feel safe, loved and like we belong. When we don't get this from our caregivers, it leads us to develop what are called 'learned behaviours'. These aren't logical behaviours, but they're more like feelings you had as a child. These are feelings such as the following (circle the feelings that resonate most with you:)

- ♥ I don't feel like I belong in this family.

- ♥ I don't feel important.

- ♥ I don't feel safe here.

- ♥ I don't feel significant.

- ♥ I don't feel I matter.

- ♥ I don't feel anyone cares for me.

- ♥ I feel different from all my friends' families.

- ♥ I don't feel like my feelings are heard, seen or acknowledged.

- ♥ I feel invisible.

- ♥ I feel like nothing I do is ever good enough.

When we feel like this, and we feel our primary needs aren't being met or that we don't belong, we learn to adapt and to take on a new role in the family. The role we take on will be one that will help us to fit it, belong and feel like we matter in the family, as we believe that, when we do, we'll be seen and heard and we'll get the love and connection we need. Which of the following four primary roles do you feel you took on?

1. The carer

This is where you took on the role of caring for everyone else whilst abandoning your own needs.

2. The overachiever

This is where you felt valued through success and achievement. You were often seen as 'the good girl' and often fixed everything as you believed you were the only one who could.

3. The difficult one or the rebel

This is where you felt seen and heard when you were difficult or acted out as that's when you got your caregivers' attention.

4. The sick one

This is where you learned that by being sick you received love and connection from your caregivers.

Looking back on your childhood in the TV screen in your mind, which one of the roles did you play?

Finish this sentence: As a child, I felt I had to take on the role of…

....

Finish this sentence: Because if I didn't, I… [some common examples are: "wouldn't be loved", "wouldn't be accepted", "wouldn't fit it", or "would be rejected".]

....
....
....

Growing up, this role you played and the behaviours you developed were a survival mechanism to ensure you remained safe and got love and connection, even if it were only breadcrumbs; however, as we grow up, leave our families and enter the world of relationships, the role you play begins to spill over into those relationships in the form of people-pleasing, co-dependency, always giving whilst others take, being sick, fixing, sabotaging or acting out to gain any breadcrumbs of love and connection.

Which of the learned behaviours are showing up in your relationships today?

....

....

....

Do you find yourself people-pleasing, fixing, sabotaging or over-giving to gain love and connection in your relationships?

....

....

....

For example, if you played the role of *the carer* growing up, you'll most likely be the carer in relationships, putting your partner's needs before your own and always being the one to give whilst your partner takes. This can become incredibly frustrating, and it can then lead to you resenting your partner, feeling stuck and feeling like you can't be yourself in relationships, as you have a deep-seated belief that you have to play the role of the carer and giver in order to get love.

These changes we make, roles we play, and behaviours and beliefs we develop all lead us to abandon completely our authentic self and our needs, but the changes happen so slowly over time that we can't even see it happening. It reminds me of the well-known story of putting a frog into a pan of cold water and then slowly increasing the heat over time until it reaches boiling point; it occurs so gradually that the frog doesn't even realise it's happening. However, if you put that same frog straight into a pot of boiling water, its initial reaction would be to jump straight out.

So why don't we jump straight out of relationships when we see red flags or feel something isn't right?

The answer is years of conditioning, years of self-abandonment to get love, and years of ingrained behaviours, beliefs, patterns and programs that all cause us to enter and stay in relationships from a place of *wound* rather than a place of worth. It's also because of conditioning that has most likely run through our families for years.

As an example from my own family, my parents also came from very large dysfunctional families: my dad is one of seven, and my mum is one of 14. How do you possibly give equal love and connection to 14 children, with each one born within around one year of the last? I remember once asking my late grandfather that very question, and his answer was that the sick ones need you the most, so it came as no surprise that the majority of the 14 children became sick at some point and the overachievers were left to get on with their own lives as the parents felt they never needed to worry about them. That the same pattern now runs through my own family of seven children.

To break the cycle, these roles, patterns, programs and beliefs need to be unlearned and relearned so you can get yourself back to the beautiful, authentic person you arrived on this planet as, where your needs matter and you're enough just as you are. This book is your invitation to do that, and in *Steps 3* and *4,* that's exactly what we'll be doing together, so get ready for some light bulb moments in the coming steps, and as you do, please remember that, by healing yourself, you're having a profound impact on the generational patterns that will carry on throughout all the future generations in your family.

First, let's consider how unhealed wounds are showing up in the present, particularly in your relationships, which is what we're going to look at in the next step.

"We attract our
unhealed wounds."

– Fiona Challis

Step 2
Attachment Styles

As humans, we have a biological need for love, connection and belonging. Our first experience of how we get this emotional bond is with our parents or primary caregivers, and research has now shown that these early relationships and our experience of how we get love and connection then go on to develop our attachment styles. These attachment styles then set the foundation for our adult and romantic relationships.

According to extensive research by John Bowlby (the founder of attachment theory and renowned British psychologist),[3] and also according to Dr Amir Levine and Rachel S.F. Heller in their phenomenal book *Attached*,[4] in which they discuss attachment styles with a particular reference to romantic relationships, they identify that we learn to get love, connection and attachment in one of these four attachment styles (or variations of them): anxious, avoidant, anxious–avoidant (fearful) or secure attachment style.

When I discovered and began to understand attachment theory, I finally began to make sense of why I was attracting a particular type of partner and why I behaved and reacted the way I did in relationships. Once I understood this, it transformed not just my romantic relationships but also my relationships with myself, my son, my work colleagues, my family and my friends. By understanding your attachment style, you'll be able to do the same, so let's delve into each of these styles so you can ultimately put an end to unhealthy relationship choices and patterns.

Anxious attachment style

If you have an anxious attachment style, your happiness will most likely depend on the quality of the relationships you're in, particularly your romantic relationships. In relationships, you're likely to have a heightened emotional intuition, may frequently be living with a sixth sense for danger, and might sometimes jump to conclusions too quickly. An example of this could be if your partner doesn't answer two or three of your texts/calls or can't meet up with you, and you then assume he's going off you or cheating on you. You fear being rejected or abandoned, which drives you to people-please, and without constant reassurance and validation, you may feel insecure and become clingy in your relationships. You're most likely highly sensitive and crave deep love and connection. In relationships, you're very often the giver, and you often put your partner's needs first, forgetting about your own. When you're in a relationship, you might also find yourself obsessively overthinking about your partner and your relationship, become consumed with thoughts of getting more closeness and connection with your partner, and have difficulty thinking about anything else. You'll probably see only the good in your partner and put him on a pedestal.

When you have an anxious attachment style, the types of partner you're prone to attracting are emotionally unavailable or broken men whom you'll rescue and fix; such men often have an avoidant attachment style, which unfortunately includes narcissists and those who create toxic relationships, as they're deeply attracted to givers in relationships. You most likely have a pattern of attracting a 'project' rather than a partner and of parenting your partner rather than making the relationship work for you. If you're unhappy in a relationship and see red flags, you'll likely ignore them, tolerate unhealthy behaviour and stay in the relationship much longer than you should as staying is less painful than letting go for you. When relationships do end, you'll be liable to find yourself stuck in heartbreak for a considerably longer time than others, as when loss happens and your attachment style is activated, you can find it incredibly hard to let go.

Avoidant attachment style

If you have an avoidant attachment style, you're most likely keep love, relationships and partners at arm's length. You're probably self-sufficient, independent and in control of all other areas of your life, but beneath it all, you may feel disconnected from your emotions.

You desire love and connection; however, you have difficulty connecting to and navigating your own emotions. This disconnect causes you to put a wall up and maintain strict boundaries. In a relationship, you may therefore appear emotionally distant, struggle with intimacy, and have a hard time opening up to your partner and maintaining those relationships. You'll be quick to see the negative characteristics of your partner, and if he becomes too needy and overdependent on you, you may find yourself pulling back. You'll tend to suppress rather than express your own needs, as you see neediness as a weakness, and you very often feel alone in relationships. You're prone to being very suspicious in relationships, and at the first sign of trouble, you may withdraw or run. When a relationship does end, you'll likely stay single for a long period of time as it feels safer for you to stay single and in control.

The types of partner you'll likely attract are those with an anxious blueprint or who are emotionally unavailable. This is because you attract what you are, and if you're unavailable to your own emotions, that's whom you'll attract. As you avoid commitment, you often attract unavailable men, married men or men who aren't ready for commitment, and this can often leave you feeling that, in relationships, you're being used. You may also find yourself being the main breadwinner/provider in relationships, which you'll like but often resent too.

Anxious–avoidant (fearful) attachment style

This attachment style has both the avoidant and anxious trademarks, which can make it very hard for women with this style, as some days you'll think you have it all sorted and everything is going great, and on other days your mind will feel like there's an inner chatter monkey in it that just won't shut up! In relationships, this attachment style reminds me of the lyrics of Katie Perry's song 'Hot N Cold', as when you're single, you'll probably crave a relationship and when you're in a relationship, you'll crave being single.

You have a huge capacity to love and connect deeply to others; however, you also have a deep-rooted fear that you'll be betrayed or taken advantage of, and you have a tendency to sabotage relationships.

The types of partner you'll likely attract are emotionally unavailable men and men who seem really into you at the start, but who then go cold on you and ghost you, resulting in you then starting to chase them and get clingy. You'll tend to also attract married or unavailable men, as they'll see they can take you or leave you, as that's the vibe you're giving off. This attachment style can also attract toxic and often painful love choices.

Secure attachment style

Having a secure attachment style in relationships means you're confident in yourself. You don't worry about rejection or lose yourself in your partner's personality. You know your boundaries and how to express them without coming off as cold. You're reliable, consistent, trustworthy and have very little drama in your romantic relationships. You're comfortable with closeness and intimacy. You're attuned to your partner's needs and know how to respond to them, but you're also clear on your own needs and values and how to communicate them. You strive for healthy and happy relationships with yourself and your partner, and you're unlikely to have negative thoughts about your relationships. You most likely have healthy self-soothing strategies and don't rely on your partner to make you happy.

The type of partner you'll most likely attract is those who're attracted to a woman who knows what she wants and is able to open up easily and share her feelings and values, as this allows them to also open up and be themselves. You'll attract a partner who's able to give and receive love, and who wants a trusting, healthy and long-term relationship. The great news is that this attachment style is like a repellent for narcissists, as they're envious and put off by secure women who're in control and self-dependent. If a relationship does end, you may be sad for a while, but you'll also know you'll be fine as you have a happy relationship with the most important person of all: yourself.

Identifying your attachment style

Most of us will have one primary attachment style, and some may have a tendency to switch to one of the other attachment styles in given situations and relationships. As an example, you may have an anxious attachment style in romantic relationships; however, as a parent, you may have a more secure attachment-style tendency.

Now you know more about attachment styles, which one do you think you have? If you're still not sure, you can also head over to **www.rapidrelationshiptherapy.com/bookresources** where I've provided a free quiz to help you quickly identify your primary attachment style.

How many of us have each of the four attachment styles? Estimates vary, but research[5] suggests that, on average, *50–60%* of people have a secure attachment style, which is great news, as there's a good chance of finding a romantic partner who can help you overcome your insecurities if you have one of the insecure attachment styles. In addition (and again, these are averages), 20–22.5% tend to have an anxious attachment style, 20–22.5% tend to have an avoidant attachment style and the remaining 5–10% tend to have an anxious–avoidant attachment style; these three styles can all be grouped together as an insecure attachment style.

In my own therapy practice, 70% of the ladies I work with have an anxious attachment style, 15% have an avoidant attachment style, and 15% have an anxious–avoidant (fearful) attachment style.

How understanding your attachment style helps you in relationships

You may be wondering how understanding your attachment style can help you to attract and keep love and to put an end to unhealthy relationship choices and patterns, so let's look at the steps to take.

Your first step is to become aware of which attachment style you have and how it shows up in your relationships, which is hopefully what you've just done. The second step is to consider what happens when each pair of attachment styles get together, so you can you see if you're compatible with each style and whether such a relationship is likely to explode with love and connection, or explode with arguments, disagreements and resentment. The third step is to take action and set boundaries in your relationships to help you overcome any insecurities and feel more secure in your relationships, which we'll cover in *Step 9*, the final step.

Now let's look at *Step 2* and what happens when each of the attachment styles gets together with others.

When you have a secure attachment style, you're more likely to attract secure partners naturally, and when you both show up as secure in your relationship, you can then successfully co-create your relationship together. However, the great news is that a secure man is also capable of having a healthy and loving relationship with both anxious- and avoidant-attachment-style women, as they're comfortable enough with themselves to give anxious types all the reassurance they need and to give avoidant types the space they need without feeling threatened themselves.

On the other hand, anxious and avoidant types end up in relationships with each other more often than they end up in relationships with their own type. When those with insecure attachment styles – such as anxious and avoidant – get together, they tend to show up in relationships with very different intentions. One shows up as very 'self-orientated', so they are incredibly focused on their own needs and wants. The other shows up as very 'others-orientated', so they're extremely focused on the wants and needs of their partner. Take a look at the following scale and see where you think you fall on it. Do you show up on the far left, as you're very others-orientated, or on the far right, as you're very self-orientated?

Others-orientated					Self-orientated				
Focus on wants and need of others					Focus on own wants and needs				
-5	-4	-3	-2	-1	+1	+2	+3	+4	+5
				Neutral Balance					

Figure 1: The co-dependent giver versus the toxic taker

It was only after reading one of the best books I found on my own journey, *The Human Magnet Syndrome* by Ross Rosenburg,[6] that I began to understand just how much those of us at opposite ends of the scale are magnetically pulled together and what the consequences of those relationships may be.

When anxious-attachment-style women get together with avoidant-attachment-style men

Through Ross Rosenburg's truly wonderful analogy of 'the dance',[7] I finally began to understand why women with an anxious attachment style get stuck in the pattern of attracting and accepting toxic or unhealthy relationships and also why we tolerate or stay in relationships even though we know they aren't good for us.

In Ross's 'the dance' analogy, he looks at how, on the far end of the self-orientated scale, you have those with narcissistic traits, where they're only focused on themselves and taking, whereas at the far end of the others-orientated scale, you have those with more co-dependency traits, where they're much more focused on others' needs and are people-pleasers, as they seek love and connection by giving and making everyone else happy.

When these two types come together in a relationship, they enter a well-matched but dysfunctional dance of romance. They can instinctively predict each other's moves. To those watching, they dance together seamlessly, almost like they've danced professionally together for years and are meant to dance together. For the purpose of explaining how the dance works, I'm going to refer to the self-focused partner as the 'toxic taker' and the others-orientated one as the 'co-dependent giver'.

The toxic taker (the man) leads and controls, and the co-dependent giver (the woman) follows his lead, making them perfectly compatible dance partners. The attraction between the pair is magnetic. He's magnetically attracted to her as she's a woman who'll give, sacrifice, and make him feel strong and in control, and he loves the attention, praise and taking centre focus. She's magnetically attracted to him as she loves a man who takes the lead and takes control, and she loves his charm, confidence and boldness. Together, they put on a truly sexy and sizzling dance of romance.

But when the music stops playing, as the co-dependent giver keeps giving, she begins to resent him, she sees him as selfish, and she feels neglected and bitter as her needs aren't being met. Whilst he loves the power, he's still controlling the dance and his dance partner's next steps, and his needs are being met, so the relationship then becomes filled with chaos, drama and conflict.

Despite this, they keep dancing, as for the co-dependent giver, following feels familiar, and she's used to giving up her power. Going right back to her earliest relationships, she continues to confuse caretaking and sacrifice with how to get love and connection, just like when she was a young child. Slowly, over time, she ends up feeling used, and her self-esteem and self-worth hit an all-time low. Sadly, he yearns for her low self-esteem and low self-worth as he craves feeling stronger and in control, and his needs are still being met.

The couple then enter what Ross calls 'the dance trap',[8] and what Dr Amir Levine and Rachel S.F. Heller call 'the anxious–avoidant trap'.[9] This is a trap because, when you fall into it, you're trapped by it, and once you're in, it's hard to break free.

In this trap, the woman wants out, but her self-esteem and self-worth are now so low, that the thought of being alone feels too painful to bear and she believes no one will ever love her, so she continues in the dysfunctional dance, stays stuck in the pattern and submits to her dysfunctional destiny.

This is, of course, unless she chooses to stop the dance and do the inner work to heal the wounds she carries from the past, so she can then begin to overcome the insecurities in her attachment style and start to transform her attachment style into a more secure one. This will allow her to have a heathier and happier relationship with herself first, and then, in turn, she'll attract healthier, happier and more secure romantic relationships.

This is what you're doing by reading this book, so if you have an anxious attachment style and the dance analogy resonates with you, congratulations for taking this first step to stop any dysfunctional dances of romance in your life.

When avoidant women get together with anxious men

Avoidant-attachment-style women will most likely keep love, relationships and partners at arm's length, but underneath – like all humans – they're wired to seek love and connection. To protect themselves and avoid relationships, many build walls so high that it appears impossible for a potential partner to climb over them, so it's very often only the anxiously attached man who's willing to stay around long enough to put in the extra effort to get the woman to open up and to break down their wall slowly, which is what magnetically draws these attachment styles together. However, like the anxious–avoidant trap we looked at earlier, these relationships can also become dysfunctional as they fall into the trap of chaser and chased, and together, they enter a feisty dance of push and pull.

With the anxious partner seeking love and intimacy and craving connection, he chases the avoidant one, but eventually, the avoidant partner starts to pull back and potentially run away as she finds it difficult to show love and intimacy, and she would rather go back to her old familiar status of being alone. As the anxious man continues to chase, the avoidantly attached women often begins to sabotage by avoiding calls and ignoring text messages. Shortly afterwards, they fall into the attachment trap, with the anxious man starting arguments as he feels his needs aren't being met, and the avoidant women sees him as smothering, overbearing and weak. She would rather be single and in control, so she rebuilds her protective wall to put more distance in the relationship.

The anxious–avoidant attachment style makes for a troubled and draining relationship because, at the core, the two have opposing approaches to love, connection and intimacy. The anxious one moves towards intimacy, love and connection, and the avoidant one moves away from intimacy, love and connection to regain her space. The anxious man needs intimacy, and the avoidant woman needs to keep her independence.

Your relationship inventory

Looking back on your past relationships through an attachment-style, informed lens, what type of partners have you been attracting?

....

....

....

Perhaps you have an anxious attachment style and have been stuck on the emotional rollercoaster of attracting avoidant men who've been taking you on their dysfunctional dance of romance? Or perhaps you have an avoidant attachment style and have been attracting anxious partners whom you find too needy and want to run? Or perhaps you're in the small percentage of women who fall into the anxious–avoidant (fearful) attachment style and have been attracting a mix of both, leaving you feeling like one day you want a relationship and the next you don't?

Doing this type of relationship inventory so you can identify your current relationship blueprint and attraction type is a crucial step in your healing, as once you can see the pattern, you can then begin to take the right next steps towards making your relationships more secure.

But what if you're already in an anxious–avoidant relationship? Can it work?

If you're already in an anxious–avoidant relationship, then yes, it can work and thrive, *but only if each party is willing to accommodate the other's emotional needs.* For example, avoidant ones may need to be patient with their partners, maintain openness and not avoid important conversations that can lead to emotional intimacy. Likewise, anxious individuals should work to overcome their insecurities and anxieties by healing their unhealed wounds, letting go and releasing fear, due to understanding that trying to control every aspect of a relationship is a form of self-sabotage. We'll explore more on how to accommodate each other's emotional needs in *Step 9* when we look at creating healthy relationship boundaries.

How to avoid the trap if you're currently single

If you're currently single or have just come out of a relationship and are struggling with heartbreak, I'd like you to consider this: is it your relationship-picker button that isn't working or your relationship-rejector button? This was a great lesson I learned from renowned relationship expert Esther Perel.[10] It was definitely my relationship-rejector button that wasn't working, as I went into relationships so fast without even stopping to think if they were right for me or not, and I ignored every red flag.

Once you become more secure in yourself, and we work out what type of relationship you want and what your boundaries are, you'll then have more confidence to hit that relationship-rejector button, which is what we're going to do in *Step 9*.

"We make our beliefs and then our beliefs make us."

– Marissa Peer

Step 3
Programming & Patterns

H A **P** P I N E S S

Whilst writing this book, I moved from the home I'd spent the previous 16 years in whilst bringing up my son. It was the only home he had ever known, as we moved in after I divorced his father when my son was three, but when he flew the nest and went to university, it just didn't feel the same to me. It felt empty, and I found walking past his bedroom every day too emotional, so I decided a change would be good for me and, as a result, made the decision to sell up and move. I'm now happily settled in our new home, and I love it.

Our old house was a Grade 2 listed building with a real water tower, as I love character buildings. It was built in 1850, and all the systems in the house – the gas, electric and heating – were very old but functioning systems. Our new house is perfect since it still has the character feel on the outside I love, but everything inside had just been newly renovated, and it has all the mod cons you'd expect to see in a brand-new house. This includes a very cosy underfloor heating system, which was incredibly appealing to me as my previous house had old stone floors, which were always very cold.

The person who lived in the new house prior to us was an elderly lady who wasn't very mobile, so she mainly lived on the ground floor, and the heating systems were only set to be on in the rooms she would be in at a certain time of day. The upper floors, which she never used unless visitors stayed over, were on minimal heating settings. Of course, when I moved in, I had to change the programming on all the systems as I planned to use all the rooms in the house.

Thankfully, her family had kept all the instruction manuals, so after moving in, I tried to change the programming to give us heating and hot water at times that suited us. However, the family didn't tell me that you'd need a PhD to be able to operate the system and update the programs. I mean, who creates these systems and instruction manuals? This one was clearly written for a professional who knows what they're doing, not in layman's terms for someone like me.

After five hours of trying and getting nowhere, I gave up and called my friend's husband, who's an engineer, to see if he could come and help me as it was clearly not my speciality. Within 30 minutes of arriving, he had all the programming updated and made it look so easy!

Whilst I was watching him to make sure I knew how to do it myself in the future, I started thinking about how, when we move house, we do a good clean out to throw away the things we no longer want or need or that no longer serve us, and we have to take the time to change the settings and update the programming in the new house to make it work for us and our needs, but when we move into a new relationship, we very rarely do this. We don't take the time to think about what we want, what works for us and our needs, and how we want the relationship to work. Instead, we very often move into a new relationship without healing previous wounds and with old programming still intact, whilst expecting a different relationship. This means we carry our wounds with us, even though they no longer serve us, along with old programming that hasn't been updated in a very long time, and as a result, the 'happy ever after' and dream of a better relationship never happen. Rather, we stay stuck in the programming of attracting and accepting unhealthy relationships.

Therefore, in this step, you're going to take the next crucial steps to identify any old programming that needs to be updated so you can set a new program to have a healthy and happy relationship with yourself and others.

What do I mean by 'programming' in relationships? Programming is a set of beliefs – and ones you've most likely formed at a very young age. These beliefs determine how you see the world, how you see yourself, and how you see and act in relationships. These beliefs play out over time and then begin to form a pattern, and as you repeat the pattern, you form your relationship programming.

As an example, when I was six years old, a neighbour walked me to school one particular day. On the walk, I vividly remember her telling me that she thought I was different, I was unlike my other siblings, and I had an older and wiser head on my shoulders for such a young girl – which isn't surprising given that I had to take on so many adult responsibilities at such a young age. But as children, we don't want to be different; we want to be the same as others so we can belong, connect with them and develop friendships, which meant developing this belief that I was different really impacted how I connected with other children. I often felt like I was the odd one out or that the other children in my class didn't like me. This wasn't true, of course; it was just a belief I'd formed as a young girl, and that belief was then carried into my future relationships, where I always felt somewhat disconnected from my partners.

How we identify your old programs

For over a year, I had a traditional talk-therapy session for 60 minutes every Friday afternoon to help me get to the real root cause of my relationship beliefs, patterns and programming, but it was only when I had a hypnosis session with an RTT therapist that I was truly able to tap into the deep-rooted beliefs I'd formed.

This is because these beliefs we form have become so deeply rooted in our subconscious minds that they're hard to access through traditional talk therapy because this type of therapy uses the conscious mind. However, hypnosis has the ability to access the subconscious mind safely and quickly; this is the part of your mind that has stored everything you've learned and experienced –

every thought, belief, pattern and program you've formed – and the real root cause of why you've developed them. By using this RTT approach, I was able to access the information I needed to resolve my relationship issues without spending years in therapy.

I was so impressed by how much this modality could help women like me to tap into, become aware of and release any destructive or negative beliefs, patterns and programs that have been keeping them stuck in destructive and unhealthy relationships that I decided to retrain in the therapy (which was founded by my mentor Marissa Peer) so I could help other women just like me to also transform and reprogram their relationship patterns, meaning they too could have happy and healthy relationships with themselves and others.

In the final part of the next step, I'll be helping you to tap into your powerful subconscious mind also, as I've created and recorded a free hypnosis session for you. This session will guide you to get to those deeply rooted beliefs that have been keeping you stuck. In the recording, I also provide a transformational experience that I'd encourage you to listen to before going to sleep – every evening for 21 days – as this will help you to let go of old programming that's no longer serving you and to reprogram your subconscious mind with more empowering beliefs to attract and maintain healthy, happy and loving relationships with yourself and others.

In the meantime, it's also important to understand your programming at a conscious level, as you can't change what you don't understand, so let's first spend some time in this step to understand where and how these deep-rooted beliefs came into your life and relationships, then we can start to reprogram your relationship patterns.

Understanding your deep-rooted beliefs

For this exercise, you'll need to grab a pen to capture any thoughts that come up whilst you reflect on some of your earlier childhood memories, which is where most of your beliefs have been formed. As in the previous step, it's important that, when reflecting, you don't relive the experience; instead, I invite you to see the picture, thoughts and feelings that come up for you as if they were on a TV screen in your mind's eye so you can revisit but not relive any memories.

It's also important to note that some women, including me, don't have many childhood memories, which makes these questions tricky to answer, so just explore what does come up. If nothing comes up, that's also fine as we'll be reviewing why this happens to you in *Step 6*.

When you're ready, I'd like you to think about the home you lived in between the ages of two and eight. If you lived in more than one place during that time, your brilliant mind will choose the right one for you. Then, in your mind's eye, I'd like you to go back to the home you've pictured. When you picture your home, I want you to open the front door, go inside, look around and see everything that's familiar to you.

Now I want you to go to the room you slept in as a child. Place your hand on the door handle, open the door and see the younger version of yourself. You recognise that child instantly as the younger version of yourself, and the child recognises you as the grown up them. The two of you have complete affinity – a perfect connection. You're going to ask the younger you some questions, and the answers will come to you immediately. Make a note of the thoughts and feelings that come up for you.

Ask her how old she is now.

....

Ask her if she's happy.

....

If she says she's happy, ask her what's making her feel happy.

....
....
....

If she says she's unhappy, ask her what someone is doing or not doing that is making her feel unhappy.

....
....
....

Now take a moment to think about what these reflections as younger you made you think, feel, believe and conclude about yourself.

Complete the following sentence:

As a child I felt...

....

....

....

Think about the beliefs you formed in your happy or unhappy memories as the younger you and make a note of them below.

....

....

....

Complete the following sentence:

As I child I believed...

....

Ask yourself how these beliefs are impacting you in your life and relationships today and make a note of them...

....

....

....

Well done!

You can now turn off the TV screen in your mind's eye and come back to the present moment so we can begin to process the thoughts, feelings and beliefs that came up for you.

By reflecting on your experiences and writing down some of your thoughts, feelings and beliefs, you can begin to identify the programming you've become conditioned to over the years.

Considering what did and didn't happen is equally important, as most people assume that it's what happens to you that forms beliefs, but it can very often be what you didn't get or what didn't happen that can cause limiting beliefs to be formed.

For many of the women I do this reflection exercise with, the most common thoughts, feelings and limiting beliefs that come up are the following:

- I felt loved by one parent but not the other.
- I felt rejected or abandoned.
- I felt like I didn't matter, was ignored or was being left out.
- I felt like what I wanted wasn't available to me.
- I felt different or like I didn't fit in.
- I felt like I wasn't seen or heard.
- I felt unsafe or scared.
- I felt I was being criticised or invalidated for my achievements or appearance.
- I felt like I had to get everything right.

This then led these same women to develop one or more of the three most common beliefs I see in women who want to change their relationship patterns, which are:

- **I'm not enough or not worthy.**
- **I'm not lovable.**
- **I'm different and can't connect with others.**

This leads to the creation of their programming on how they approach and act in relationships. For most, this means they're approaching relationships from a place of being wounded rather than a place of worth, and they're therefore attracting and accepting unhealthy and unsafe relationships.

This all leads to these women forming even more disempowering beliefs about men, relationships and love.

As an exercise, read the following prompts and then complete the sentences with the words you hear yourself say and the pictures or feelings that come up for you. Just trust what comes up.

Men are...

....

Love is...

....

Relationships are...

....

When I run this exercise in my group coaching programs, the following sections give some of the most common answers that come up.

Men

- Men are hurtful.
- Men are liars.
- Men are weak.
- Men are cheats.
- Men are unreliable.
- Men are unable to be trusted.

Love

- Love is hurtful.
- Love is not available to me.
- Love is not for me.

Relationships

- Relationships are not worth it.
- Relationships are something that never works out for me.
- Relationships are hard work.
- Relationships are challenging.

Based on the pictures they paint and the words they're saying to themselves, the women I work with then form even more disempowering beliefs. They almost always expect things to go wrong or be difficult in relationships because – at a deep, core level – they have all these limiting beliefs holding them back, keeping them stuck or blocking love. When relationships inevitably end, this further builds on their beliefs that they mustn't be enough, they're unworthy or unlovable, or there's something wrong with them.

However, there's nothing wrong with them and they aren't broken. They're simply approaching love and relationships with a set of outdated beliefs that haven't been updated or reprogrammed in a very long time.

Likewise, there's nothing wrong with you and you aren't broken. You've simply been entering relationships with a set of outdated beliefs.

Take a moment to reflect on any outdated beliefs and programming you've been approaching relationships with. Write them in the space on the next page.

Outdated beliefs

"By changing nothing,
nothing changes."

– Tony Robbins

Step 4
Protector Parts

When all those beliefs, words and pictures we identified in the previous step come together, they form a part within you, almost like a layer or wall, that keeps all these limiting beliefs locked inside you and covers up the real you – the authentic person you are whom these beliefs have disconnected you from, the truly lovable person and the person who was perfect just as you were when you arrived on this planet.

Let's cast our minds back to the authentic you.

An analogy I like to use with my clients to help them get back to their authentic self is to ask them (and you) to imagine seeing themself (yourself) as a beautiful, shiny diamond, which sparkles, is pure, is raw, is authentic and is priceless.

Identifying your limiting beliefs

Over the years, those limiting beliefs we've just identified start to cover, piece by piece, the shiny diamond that you are. They cover your personality, dim your brightness, and before you know it, this beautiful, shiny diamond has been completely covered up with all these limiting beliefs. It happens so slowly that you don't consciously see it occurring, in a similar way to the story in *Step 3* of the frog in the pan of cold water that heats up slowly over time until the frog boils.

What beliefs have you put over yourself to hide the shiny diamond you are – that treasure inside you?

....

....

....

What beliefs have you put over yourself that have dimmed your brightness and prevented you from shining and being the real you – not the one who shows up in relationships sometimes, but the authentic you? Because that's what those negative beliefs do: they stop you from shining, and they stop you from being the real you.

If you've ever been in a relationship and thought, *If they see the real me, they might leave me,* or, *I wish I could just be myself in relationships or meet someone that I can be my authentic self with,* then this is your shiny diamond trying to break free and radiate brightness. However, the low self-esteem and low self-worth that has probably covered the diamond for many years is preventing you having the confidence to be the real you.

This part of you covering the shiny diamond is the part that shows up in your relationships today. It's the part of you that stops the real you from coming out. In some cases, this part forces you to shut down. You shut down to love and you think it's safer to stay single. It keeps you stuck in repetitive cycles as this part of you thinks remaining in the old familiar pattern is keeping you safe. It's preventing you both giving and receiving true love; it's preventing you letting go and letting love in.

If, whilst in a relationship, you've ever found yourself thinking part of you wants the relationship and part of you doesn't, or part of you wants love and part of you doesn't, this is the part I'm referring to.

This part of you sits deep within your subconscious mind, and when this part came into your life, it thought it had a good role, a good function, a good purpose and a good intention. It had a job description, which was to keep you safe and do what you told it to do. But here's the problem: this part came into your life at a very young age and what it needed to do to keep you safe back then is no longer what it needs to do today.

It's still playing a role and turning up every day, but it's doing its job based on a job description that's perhaps 20, 30 or 40 years old. It just doesn't know it yet because you haven't updated the job spec. So today, we're going to give that part of you a voice, so we can find out the following:

- What was it trying to do when it came into your life?
- What does it think its role or job is?
- When did it come into your life?

We then need to upgrade it. Think of it this way: if you were running a company, you wouldn't have the same job specification for both somebody you hired 36 years ago and somebody you hired today, would you?

You should see this part of you as a loyal employee who's playing a role within you, but it's playing that role with a completely outdated job spec. Everything in that job spec needs to be upgraded. It needs to be reprogrammed so it serves you as the grown woman you are today.

Meet your protector parts

To access this part of you, we need to tap into your subconscious mind safely and quickly, as this is where this part of you is deeply rooted. When you're ready, you can now listen to the free hypnosis session that accompanies this book, so we can then meet this part of you, give it a voice and give it a new role that will help you to transform any disempowering beliefs we've identified in this step into more empowering beliefs.

This is a really important part of your healing journey, and just like you accept and schedule time for your mobile phone to get a software update when you get the alert, please take this as your alert to schedule some time for yourself so we can begin the process of upgrading the role this part is playing in your life and relationships today.

Your free hypnosis session with Fiona

The hypnosis session lasts for 30 minutes, and I suggest you listen to the session each day for 21 days (in the evening before you go to bed), as the powerful, transformational experience I've included will help you to reprogram your thoughts, beliefs and patterns, so you can have truly healthy, happy and loving relationships going forward.

You can find this session* at **www.rapidrelationshiptherapy. com/bookresources**; I hope you enjoy it.

* Disclaimer: Please do not listen to this hypnosis session if you're driving, suffer from epilepsy or have any form of psychosis.

"The cry we hear from deep in our hearts comes from the wounded child within. Healing this inner child's pain is the key healing to transforming anger, sadness, and fear."

– Thich Nhat Hanh

Step 5
Meeting Your Inner Child

When I was doing my own inner work, I came across a truly beautiful story. It's a story about a monastery in Thailand. In 1957, the entire monastery was being relocated, and a group of monks were put in charge of moving a giant clay Buddha. In the midst of the move, one of the monks noticed a crack in the Buddha and became concerned about damaging the idol, so they decided to wait a day before continuing with their task.

Later, one of the monks came to check on the giant statue. He shone his flashlight over the entire Buddha, and when he reached the crack, he saw something reflected back at him. His curiosity aroused, the monk got a hammer and a chisel and began chipping away carefully at the clay Buddha. As he knocked off piece after piece of clay, the Buddha got brighter and brighter. After hours of work, the monk looked up in amazement to see a huge, solid-gold Buddha standing before him.

Historians believe the Buddha had been covered with clay by monks several hundred years earlier, before an attack by the Burmese army, so they could protect the Buddha. All the monks were killed in the attack, so it wasn't until 1957 that the great treasure was discovered. Today, the statue resides in the Temple of the Golden Buddha in Bangkok, Thailand. It stands 10 feet tall and weighs in excess of 5.5 tons. It's made of solid pure gold, and today's valuation of it is to the tune of $200 million.

This story resonated with me because, like the Buddha, our outer shell protects us from the world as we see it, but our real treasure is hidden within. As women, we unconsciously hide our inner gold under a layer of clay. The heaviest layer of clay is from our own limiting beliefs, patterns and programs that we formed through the eyes of a young child, so as to protect us. The other layers of clay have accumulated over time, through external conditioning from our parents, schools, and teachers and from our relationships and the meanings we attach to them. We all have our own story that sits beneath our protective layer of clay, but it's when we have the courage to chip away at that clay, as we did in the last step and will continue to do in this one, that we uncover our gold and reconnect with the true treasure that has been sitting inside us all this time.

Let's now meet the true treasure that has been within you all this time; let's meet your inner child.

Meeting your inner child

Meeting your inner child starts by accepting that we all have an inner child within us. It's not separate to us, which I used believe before doing this work, but it's a part of us that still lives with us daily during our adult lives. We normally meet our inner child when we're in relationships. We meet them when we're wounded, as that reveals the inner child's wounds we're carrying. We meet them when we feel loved, appreciated, seen and heard, as that's what they perhaps dreamed about when they were growing up. We're just not consciously aware that we're meeting our inner child until we start to understand and acknowledge the wounds and desires they carry.

Here are some signs that your inner child's still wounded and showing up in your relationships:

- You feel anxious around other people who're loud, obnoxious, or show little consideration, regard or empathy for others.

- You're very sensitive to people accusing you of things or where you feel an injustice has been done to you.

- You're highly agreeable and do whatever it takes to please others.

- You think that your partners should automatically know what you want and need.

- You care for others and therefore expect others to meet your needs.

- You subjugate your own needs.
- You don't have clear boundaries.
- You don't take care of yourself.
- You feel like you need to be heard and you fight to be understood by others.
- You find yourself constantly ruminating over people or situations.
- Happy people annoy you, and you get upset when others have what you want.
- You always support the underdog and at the expense of yourself.
- You feel unable to trust others and think others are out to hurt you.
- You criticise yourself, judge yourself and compare yourself to others.
- You generally feel disappointed with people.
- You feel unsafe around others.
- You find yourself on guard constantly and think others are out to get you.
- You're highly suspicious of others.
- You feel like others don't want you around and nobody loves you.
- You dissociate, isolate or shut down when others get angry.
- You feel responsible for fixing everything and everybody.

Do any of these resonate with you? If so, these are inner child wounds that are being activated.

How my inner child showed up in my romantic relationships

In *Step 1*, I shared that, growing up, I used to love watching the TV show called *The Waltons*, and for the 60 minutes of the show, I'd escape into this fantasy world of being part of a loving family, living in a beautiful house with a white picket fence. As I got older, I got hooked on another show called *Dallas*, and again, I'd escape and pretend that I was married to Bobby Ewing, the nicest of the brothers in the show. I'd very often dream, fantasise and write about how my life was going to be when I grew up. But it was only when I started therapy and explained to my therapist that my childhood wasn't that bad and I didn't really have many childhood memories apart from my fantasies that it became clear what I'd been doing. My inner child had become so disassociated with what was going on in the present and was instead using the future fantasies as a coping mechanism to escape my reality.

Fast forward to my romantic relationships, and the same pattern appeared. I'd frequently minimise any struggles in those relationships, ignore any red flags I saw and dissociate from what was really going on in the relationship, as I'd be fantasising and planning how we'd live in a beautiful house with a white picket fence like the Waltons had, where we'd go on holiday, how we'd get married, and how we'd live a picture-perfect, happy life.

Of course, that never happened, and it was only on my wedding day that the reality hit me, and the adult in me finally got back in the driving seat and started to question whether I was making the right decision in getting married to him. It wasn't, and I knew that inside, but it was too late to change my mind. The fact we stayed together for 10 years is a miracle, as in all honesty, we had absolutely nothing in common. My family would tell me frequently that he was always putting me down and it wasn't right how he spoke to me, but of course, I couldn't see it at the time and always made excuses for him. It was only when I was in labour with our son and my husband said he was going to bed to get some sleep so he wouldn't be tired tomorrow and I should wake him up when I wanted to go back to the hospital that I finally woke up and thought, *What a selfish shit!* Here I was, in agony with contractions, trying to soothe myself by having a bath, and he was sleeping! He was there for the final part of the labour and the delivery of our son in hospital, but this was after hours of painful contractions at home with no husband to support me. I carried on as usual afterwards and was so delighted that I finally had my son and my happy family that I didn't even bring the situation up in conversation with him afterwards.

But my happy family didn't quite turn out like the Waltons; instead, I felt like a single parent, and my husband would spend most of his free time working on his cars, doing the garden or playing online poker, whilst my son and I did everything together. It was Mother's Day in 2007 when I finally cracked and told him I wanted a divorce, as I didn't want our son growing up thinking this was what love and a happy marriage looked like.

Six months later, I left, and my son and I started a new life in a new house. Thankfully for my son, leaving his father was the best decision I made for him, as when he went to see his father every other weekend, his father had to spend time with him, and today, they have a lovely relationship.

After killing each other for the first year after we split, my ex-husband and I both made a decision to put our son first, stay friends and create a secure family unit between us for our son, which we did do, thankfully. It wasn't the conventional Waltons-style family unit, but it worked as we were both always there for our son; he always felt loved, secure and safe; and he always had two parents at every school meeting, football match or party, despite us being divorced.

After my marriage ended, I met a guy called Chris, who was from South Africa. We fell in love quickly; I was the love of his life, and he was mine. He was a director, very successful in his field, gorgeous, so much fun and so loving. Although he lived there and I lived in the UK, we saw each other frequently, and each day spoke multiple times on the phone or on text messages. He was always planning how we'd all move and live in South Africa together, which I loved as it sounded and felt picture-perfect.

Almost one year after meeting him, a parcel for me was delivered to my work. When I opened it, my heart sank, as in the box were every present, letter and photo I'd ever sent him. I couldn't figure out what was going on. There was a letter in there addressed to the nickname he used to call me. I opened it, and after reading it, I fell to the floor in shock. In the letter, he explained he hadn't been honest with me and, for the last year, he'd been in marriage counselling with his wife. He said he felt so bad for lying to us both that he'd received a calling from God – I kid you not, that's what he said – and he was going to become a preacher to seek forgiveness for his sins. Despite frantically calling, texting and emailing, I never heard from him again. My happy ever after had become a horror story, and my abandonment wound had well and truly been opened.

Years later, I started dating again. I met Wes, an incredibly handsome American investment banker whom I met in Africa whilst we were both working there. When you think of Bobby Ewing in *Dallas*, that's exactly what Wes was like. My colleagues who were also in Africa with me tried to warn me about him, as they thought he was lying to me and simply using me, but of course, I didn't listen again – not until a year later when I introduced him to my son. I suddenly saw him through the lens of an adult and mother, and something told me he wasn't to be trusted. It turned out he couldn't be, so I ended the relationship shortly afterwards.

I then met Jonathan through a coaching program I was on; he'd been the owner of the company, which he'd just sold when we met, so we spent the night celebrating and drinking champagne. We ended up seeing a lot of each other, although I felt it was always me chasing him, and even worked together on a few occasions. I thought we were an item, but he didn't, which I found out when we were both speaking at an event together, and he introduced me to his new girlfriend, whom I had absolutely no idea about! I felt like the floor had opened up and I was being sucked into the deepest black hole ever when he introduced me to her. I still don't know how I managed to speak on stage that day.

Next, there was Nigel, whom I met through an online dating site. He was a lot older than me, but I found his older look quite distinguished; that was until I felt ready to introduce him to my family and friends, including my son, and they thought he was more like my father than a partner.

After Nigel, there was John, whom I was introduced to through friends. He was the most sensible one of my exes, and there was absolutely nothing wrong with him, but he bored me. Looking back, he was way too normal for me, as I'd become so accustomed to chaos and drama in my relationships.

Then there was Seamus, whom I met in a crowded bar in Paris; he was the catalyst for me starting on my healing journey. I'll never forget the moment I felt the villa keys hit me when he threw them at me in Ibiza, as it took me right back to being that frightened young girl who frequently witnessed my father hitting my mother. I remember bystanders in the street looking at me with the same look of pity that everyone used to give us as children living in a dysfunctional home with domestic violence, and in that very moment, I made the decision to leave him as I wasn't prepared to live the life my mother had experienced with my father.

I'm sharing my story with you in this step because, in all my relationships, I was attracting my unhealed inner child wounds. I was attracting men, just like my father, and when they abandoned me, my abandonment wound from my father was well and truly opened again. I was attracting emotionally unavailable men, just like my mother did, and I'd do everything in the relationship, including putting my own needs aside to meet their needs so as to get their love and connection. I met avoidant-attachment-style men who wouldn't commit, but my anxious attachment style ignored all of the signs and instead lived in a fantasy world of how happy we'd be. I ignored every red flag I saw, as I was looking at these relationships through the eyes of a hurt young girl who just wanted to be swept off her feet and have the happy ever after.

It was my hurt inner child that was showing up in my relationships, and the only time the adult in me got back in the driving seat was when I introduced my partners to my son. When I looked at the relationships through the eyes of an adult and mother, I knew these relationships weren't right for me or my son.

Identifying how your inner child shows up in relationships

It's often only when we look back at our relationships that we can see where our inner child wounds are showing up, so let's take a look at where and how she comes up in your relationships, which will reveal the clay we need to chip away at courageously to find the true gold inside. So when you're ready, grab a pen, and as in the previous steps, read the following prompts and select any answers that apply or just finish the sentence with whatever comes to mind for you, as appropriate to the prompt. If nothing comes up for you, that's also fine.

In the previous step, we looked at the role we played to fit in and belong growing up. Which of these four roles did you take on?

- ♥ **The carer** – the one who cared for everyone else's needs and neglected their own

- ♥ **The overachiever** – the one who got love and connection through success, fixing and being the 'good girl'

- ♥ **The sick one** – the one who got the most love and connection when they were sick

- ♥ **The difficult one** – the one who got more attention and connection when they acted out

In your current and past romantic relationships, which of roles did your partners have?

- ♥ The carer

- ♥ The overachiever

- ♥ The sick one

- ♥ The difficult one

How did playing this role help you feel seen, heard and loved?

....

....

....

(As an example, many of the women I work with who played the role of carer growing up tend to be attracted to partners who have been or are sick, either physically or mentally, as they feel seen, heard and loved when they take on the role of the carer. However, later in the relationship, they may start to feel resentful as they feel like they're a parent rather than a partner.)

What's your primary attachment style? And what primary attachment styles do your current or past partners have?

You	Your Partner
Secure	Secure
Anxious	Anxious
Avoidant	Avoidant
Anxious–avoidant (fearful)	Anxious–avoidant (fearful)

In relationships, when you feel stressed or feel your needs aren't being met, which of the following coping strategies do you turn to?

- ♥ People-pleasing

- ♥ Over-giving

- ♥ Acting out or acting defensively

- ♥ Getting angry

- ♥ Dissociating

- ♥ Shutting down or giving the silent treatment

In relationships, to get love and connection I tend to...

....

....

....

Where do you primarily seek love from?

- ♥ Internally

- ♥ Externally

In relationships, I feel activated when… [Select all that apply]

- ♥ I feel unsafe
- ♥ I feel my needs aren't being met
- ♥ I feel I'm not seen and heard
- ♥ I feel I'm not loved
- ♥ I feel taken advantage off
- ♥ Others around me could be unsafe

What are the character traits of people who trigger you?

....
....
....

What words or phrases do they use that activate you?

....
....
....

Whom does this type of person remind you of from your childhood?

....
....
....

What are you most afraid of in your relationships?

....

....

....

What do you dream about having in relationships?

....

....

....

Which of the following do you do when your wounded inner child is activated or you feel triggered?

- ♥ Disassociate

- ♥ Fantasise

- ♥ Throw a tantrum

- ♥ Take the moral high ground

- ♥ Sulk and give the silent treatment

- ♥ People-please

- ♥ Blame, criticise or judge

- ♥ Compare myself and my relationship to others

What recurrent patterns do you see in your relationships?

....

....

....

The answers you've written will show you when your inner child appears in your relationships and the wounds or wants they're currently carrying. So, try to summarise them by completing the following sentences, as this will really help you on the next step when we meet your inner child.

My inner child appears in my relationships when…

....

....

....

As an example, let's use my relationship story that sat beneath my clay:

- I played the overachiever role. I was like a superwoman: doing everything and fixing everything.
- I had an anxious attachment style and always attracted avoidant partners. Even when others tried to tell me a partner wasn't right for me, I ignored this and started dreaming about our life together instead.

- When I was triggered in relationships, I dissociated or fantasised.

- I tolerated unacceptable and unhealthy behaviours, as I'd had to accept these from others as a child.

- I was always giving, and they were always taking.

- I was always seeking love externally in relationships and dreamed about who would make me happy.

- I felt activated in relationships when others around me were unsafe, hence my adult self kicking in when I introduced my partners to my son.

- I was triggered in relationships when men drank too much or raised their voices, just as I'd been triggered as a child.

- I was triggered when my partners didn't show appreciation for everything I was doing for them.

It was only through doing this work that I realised just how much my inner child was showing up in my relationships, and when I understood it was a young child under the age of nine making most of the decisions in my relationships, I was finally able to begin to make sense of my previous relationships' patterns.

Healing your inner child wounds

How can you heal some of your inner child wounds or acknowledge her wants?

You need to meet with and speak to your inner child so she feels seen, heard and loved. Not by a partner or by being in a relationship but by being seen, heard and loved by you, and by you now taking the parent role and being the parent you wished you'd had when you were growing up. This is called 'reparenting'.

To meet and speak with your inner child, I'm going to walk you through the following journalling exercise and short visualisation exercise and, based some very impactful RTT interventions taught to me my mentor Marissa Peer. Using these interventions, I was able to bring my younger self to a place of safety, and she's now with me every day, getting the love and connection she needs in the way that every child should receive love.

Inner child guided visualisation with Fiona

However, if you prefer to do a guided visualisation, you can also visit **www.rapidrelationshiptherapy.com/bookresources** to access one with me.

Upgrading your inner child

Let's now start the journalling exercise to upgrade your child, making her feel safe, seen, heard and loved by you, and so she knows you'll be the one looking out for her now. To do this exercise, it's helpful to have a photo of your younger self, somewhere when you were under the age of nine. If you have a photo, please place it in front of you whilst reading the rest of this step. If you don't have a printed or digital photo, that's also fine, just try to picture your younger self in your mind.

When you have the picture, I want you, as the adult you are now, to tell her this, either by journalling or saying the words out loud:

I'm upgrading you; you're no longer a dependent child or dependant on anyone else for love and connection, as I have you now and I'll always have you.

You've been so brave in taking on the role of... [finish with the role you played]

....

....

....

I know you felt you needed to… [write or say how your younger self got love and connection]

....

....

....

And you've been so good at looking after me, but you've done enough now and you don't need to do this anymore because I can look after us now and you are safe with me.

You're allowed to just be you, and you're allowed to be the authentic you, just as you were when you arrived on this planet.

I love you just as you are, and I promise others will still love you just as you are.

I'll give you the love, encouragement and praise you've always wanted.

Whatever you wanted to hear, needed to hear and have been waiting to hear, I'll tell you.

I'll tell you just how lovable you are, how I love your uniqueness, how you're enough just as you are and how worthy it feels to have you on this journey of life with me.

Becoming the loving parent

Now let's do the visualisation exercise. I'd like you to imagine you're holding that smaller, younger version of yourself by her hand, and then I want you to pick her up in your arms.

Take a moment to get the visualisation or feeling of picking your younger self up.

Now take your arms and wrap them around your younger self and repeat this after me:

I'm becoming the loving parent to you now.

Growing up, you might not always have felt seen, heard or loved by our parents, but I'm becoming that parent for you now.

I love you exactly the way you are.

I love you completely and unconditionally.

I'll always have time for you.

I'll always listen to you.

I've created a place in my heart and in my life just for you.

You'll always be safe with me.

You'll always be significant to me.

You're enough! You always have been and you always will be.

Everything is available to you.

You and I have balance now.

Reparenting your inner child

I'd now like you to imagine transporting your inner child to the home where you live today as an adult or to a place you see as your happy place.

Sit down with little you and repeat this after me:

You live in my world now and you're part of my world.

This is where you live from today onwards.

Wherever I go, you'll be safe and with me.

Now imagine showing younger you around your home. Show her the different rooms; show her your pictures of the life you have and the people in it; and tell her about your achievements, the freedom you have and what you do for a living. Show her all the things that weren't available to her growing up – perhaps a TV, computer, room of her own, money or lovely clothes.

Merging your inner child

Finally, I want you to imagine that younger you is hovering just above your head. I want you to picture her descending slowly, dropping down, merging into your body and melting into your heart. See her as fully embedded in your life now. She can never go back because she's taking up residence with adult you now. She is free, the past is behind her, and you're her loving parent now.

You have unconditional love for each other, and you make space together daily to ensure you feel heard, seen and loved.

Summary

Every child is born with a connection to their authentic self, but as we talked about at the start of this step, we become disconnected from ourselves and the world around us. Our beliefs and conditioning form a protective layer of clay around us until we have the courage to shine a light inside ourselves, chip away at the clay, uncover our gold, and reconnect with our inner child and authentic self.

I hope that, from the work we've done so far in this book, you are starting to feel more like the authentic you again. To deepen that connection with your inner authentic self, I'd encourage you to keep with you the photo of younger you that you used in the exercise, so she always knows that she's with you, and she's seen, heard and loved by you. I still have a photo of younger me on my fridge at home and as a screensaver on my phone. If you think that might also work for you, then give it a try.

"Trauma is not about the event. It is about the individual's response. *It's disrespectful to not understand that an individual's nervous system is making an unconscious evaluation of life threat. It's* not conscious *and it's* not voluntary. *It's the body's reaction."*

– Stephen Porges

Step 6
Nervous-system Regulation

At this stage in my healing journey, I felt like I had so many of the answers I'd been searching for. My relationship blueprint that had formed over the years was finally starting to make sense.

I'd discovered that, to fit in and belong growing up, I played the role of the overachiever, constantly trying to impress, fix and rescue others; I was confusing love with overachieving and giving. I understood why I had very few memories from my childhood, why I dissociated so much from the present, and how I used always being in my own fantasy world and thinking about what my life would be like when I grew up as a coping strategy. I'd discovered I had a primary attachment style of anxious and a secondary attachment style of avoidant in given situations, and I realised just how much I'd been seeking love and connection externally instead of looking within myself. I found that my inner child – who was holding many disempowering beliefs, patterns and programs – had been showing up in my relationships much more than I ever thought, and my adult self only came into play when I felt my son or other people around me could be put in danger.

I unearthed so much about myself that I'd had no clue about previously. When I realised just how much I'd become disconnected from myself, it filled me with a deep sadness. I wanted to take the old version of me and give her a great big hug as she'd been through so much pain and hurt.

I felt it was now time to put the past behind me. I'd chipped the clay away and felt I'd once again come home to me – the authentic me. I felt so excited, so aligned and so positive about my future, and I was excited to start dating again. I was making all of these great new plans for the next phase of my life, and I even set myself up on an internet dating site to get back out into the dating scene, but when it came to actually implementing the plans or going on a date, something inside me still felt stuck.

I couldn't understand it or explain it. I'd done so much inner work and really couldn't understand why I was still feeling stuck. It was like being trapped in quicksand; I was trying so hard to get out and move forwards, but I felt completely stuck, so I found myself back asking the same question that I asked at the very start of this book: *What's wrong with me?*

Why we feel stuck

It wasn't until I came across the new research on polyvagel theory – founded by Stephen Porges, an American psychologist and neuroscientist – that I realised there was nothing wrong with me. In fact, everything was right with me.

His research[11] illustrates how trauma affects our bodies alongside our minds, and under this framework, trauma is no longer solely defined by the event that happened but is also defined by the impact it has, specifically on our nervous system, which results from being overwhelmed and under-supported in the face of all types of overwhelming experiences. This includes relationship break-ups and the trauma experienced in current or past relationships, and I'd experienced my fair share of that.

I'd done so much inner work on my mind and heart, but I never realised until I read about this that our ability to tolerate stress and take on new challenges – such as starting to date again – depends on the functioning of our nervous system and, in particular, the functioning of the vagus nerve. I'd never even heard of the vagus nerve before, but it's quite an important one as it runs from a person's brain to all of their organs, facilitating communication between all parts of their body after a stressful event has passed. A healthy, functioning vagus nerve tells the nervous system that it's safe to relax now and move forwards, but when we haven't shown this to our body or we don't have safe and secure relationships to help us fully process difficult events, the vagus nerve doesn't send that message as it still thinks we're unsafe. As a result, our nervous system stays activated, and we enter or remain in a state of dysregulation, which is why I felt so stuck and couldn't move forwards.

Think of a time in your life when you faced an overwhelming relationship experience and you tried to move forwards or overcome a challenge in a relationship. How did your body react? Here are some of the common feelings that are signs your body is in a state of dysregulation:

- Dissociation
- Overwhelm
- Overthinking
- Anxiety
- Worry
- Frustration
- Panic
- Frozen
- Apathy
- Disinterest
- Shut down
- Disconnection
- Burnout
- Rage
- Extreme fatigue

- Fear
- Confusion
- Brain fog
- Agitation

As you've probably gathered throughout this book, when my body and nervous system becomes overwhelmed and dysregulated, I dissociate and disconnect. What answers came up for you?

....

....

....

When I first heard about dysregulation, I thought it sounded quite negative, but when I understood more about it, I could see that dysregulation is actually our system trying to protect us; it's protecting us from what it perceives as danger and from what it doesn't yet know is safe. The important word here is 'perceived', as it's when our system perceives we're unsafe that it dysregulates.

Let's have a look at what it perceives as danger and how it perceives danger, as we can then look at ways to show it we're safe in a language it understands, so we can become regulated and move forwards.

I'm going to explain this concept in layman's term so it's super easy for you to understand. (Think back to the issue with the complex instruction manual when I was trying to change the heating systems in my new house – I'm trying to avoid that here.)

First, let's look at what it perceives as danger. A simple way to look at this is that, when you have an experience in your life or relationships, your system does the equivalent of googling the same or a similar situation so it can see whether that experience was safe or unsafe previously.

As an example, I was attacked by a dog when I was three years old, and I've since developed a terrible fear of dogs because my system has classified dogs as dangerous, so when I see one, my system tells me to run, as it still perceives dogs as dangerous. As a result of this, any time I go for a walk, my self-protective system is always on high alert as it's looking to protect me. This may not seem like a traumatic experience to people who love dogs, but to my system, it is traumatic, and my body still hasn't released that trauma, and it will therefore always see dogs as a threat.

Unlike animals, who have built-in systems to help them to release trauma quickly after it happens, we hold on to trauma, and then it becomes stored and locked in time. This means our systems think the trauma is still happening in the here and now or it could happen again at any moment.

Hence, releasing trauma is an important part of healing, as without releasing it, that threat is always going to be there for us. A great example of how animals release trauma quickly is when you watch a wildlife show and you see an animal in the wild getting attacked; once the attacking animal is out of sight and the perceived danger has gone, you'll always see animals completely shake out their bodies. This whole-body shaking is their system's very clever way of releasing trauma rapidly so it doesn't become stored in their body. After the trauma has been released, they carry on grazing happily as if nothing had happened.

To bring it back to relationships, my experience with my ex Seamus throwing the villa keys at me, which hit me, sent an alert to my system to say, "This is dangerous." My system perceived it as dangerous because it was still holding on to the traumatic experience of my father's violence in our home, so when it did the equivalent of googling and confirmed the situation was dangerous, it told me to run – and I did. My autonomic nervous system came online to protect me in the form of dysregulation or active self-protection, because my past trauma of my father's violence had never been released.

When you think about it, our systems are bloody awesome! It's like we have an invisible team of nervous-system ninjas inside us that are there to always protect and guide us.

Thinking about your own life and relationships, where's your team of nervous-system ninjas trying to protect you? It could perhaps be one or more of the following:

- With men, because they perceive men as dangerous.
- With intimacy, as they perceive intimacy as dangerous.
- When you speak up, as when you tried to speak up in the past, you were shut down.
- When you try to open up or talk about your feelings, as they perceive talking about feelings as unsafe.

- With money, as they perceive stored trauma around money.
- In keeping yourself small, as being seen was dangerous growing up.

Now let's look at how your system identifies if something is a threat or not.

I want you to imagine that your system has a very loyal security guard – called neuroception – sitting outside its door. When something or someone comes to its door, your security guard googles for similar experiences or trauma stored in your body and mind, and they scan externally for any signs of danger – for example, a gut instinct that something doesn't feel right or an angry look on your partner's face – before deciding if it's safe for them to come in. When your security guard is running their search, they're checking in with your body, with your mind and externally to see if it's safe, dangerous or life-threatening. If the search result comes back as it being unsafe or dangerous, your security guard hits a big, red danger button and sets off the alarm that sends you into one of four stress responses: flight, fight, freeze or fawn.

Let's look at what each stress response looks and feels like:

- **Flight** – when your system can't see any potential way out of danger, it's going to send you into a flight response and tell you to run. This is what happened with my ex Seamus.
- **Fight** – when it thinks there may be an opportunity to win and get back to safety, it will fight.

- **Freeze** – when it can't find a way for you to get back to safety, it will jump in and freeze you in time so you don't experience the trauma. I spent a lot of my childhood here, and hence my lack of childhood memories.

- **Fawn** – when it feels you can get back to safety through people-pleasing or you can talk your way back to safety.

Which stress response do you find yourself in the most?

....

Your security guard then calls in your autonomic nervous system, or team of nervous-system ninjas, to help, which they do by assessing the person or situation, and then they'll either put you in a regulated state (if they feel you're safe and secure) or a dysregulated state (if they feel you're still unsafe). The three primary states your team of nervous-system ninjas choose from are the ventral vagal complex, sympathetic nervous system and dorsal ventral complex. There's also the freeze state, which is a blend of your sympathetic nervous system and dorsal ventral complex.

These are all very complicated names, so let me share what it feels like to be in each of these states, and honestly, when I learned about each of these states, it was as if I'd found the missing link in my healing, and I finally began to understand why I was feeling so stuck despite all the work I'd done. By understanding these feelings, it will be easier for you to work out which state(s) your nervous system is keeping you in.

Ventral vagal complex

This is our state of safety. The ventral vagal complex is the most regulated of the three states and the one that, ideally, we want to be in all the time or at least the majority of the time, as this is when we feel safe, secure and loved. In this state, you'll feel the following:

- Safe in yourself and the world
- Anchored in the present moment
- Capable and able
- Safe to make mistakes and safe to be yourself
- Full of creativity and play
- Content and in flow with yourself
- Aligned in both body and mind
- That you have a purpose, passion and goals
- Full of empathy and compassion
- Full of energy but not over-stimulated
- Connected to yourself and others
- Grounded
- Great in your body, mind and spirit

This is the overall experience that embodies what I've been working towards over the last year, and when you complete this book in its entirety, my hope is that it will guide you towards this regulated state so you can live a life of purpose, love like you've never loved before, and be happier and more content in yourself and with life.

Sympathetic nervous system

This is our state of mobilisation. Being in the sympathetic-nervous-system state can feel a bit overwhelming as there's always a sense of urgency to get things done in this state. It will use every ounce of energy in your body as it sends a message to all the other organs in your body to tell them it needs all your energy to stay in this state and keep you safe. If you've ever seen someone act with an almost superhuman power, such as in rescuing someone from a burning building, that's what this state is like. But in addition to being in something like a superhuman state, there's always a sense of urgency, so you might feel or experience one or more of the following:

- Increased adrenaline and cortisol, and a heightened alertness in all your senses
- Laser-focused vision
- Always being on the go
- Over-functioning
- Difficulty relaxing or slowing down
- A need to control external circumstances
- A burst of energy followed by fatigue
- A heightened sense of concern or worry
- Agitation
- Anxiousness
- Frustration if things don't happen as you want
- Panic and, potentially, panic attacks

- Increased heart rate
- Tightness or rigidity
- Being unable to settle easily and fidgeting
- Overly busy mind

If you're in either a fight or flight stress response, you're likely to be in this state.

Dorsal ventral complex

Our dorsal ventral complex is the polar opposite of the sympathetic nervous system. If your system thinks you're in life-threatening danger, this is the state it will place you in, as it wants to keep us safe and alive. Here, you might feel or experience one or more of these:

- Dissociated
- Apathetic
- Stuck
- Spaced out
- Disconnected
- Removed from what's going on around you
- Depressed
- Hopeless
- Shut down
- Like you're not in your own body
- Low energy

- Difficulty focusing
- Flat
- Incapable
- Shallow, slow breathing
- Brain fog
- No energy for exercise
- Heaviness

In this state, it's like your body is preparing to go into hibernation. It's getting you ready to shut down.

Freeze

This state is equal parts sympathetic nervous system and dorsal ventral complex. You might feel a bit like a deer caught in the headlights, as you don't know where to turn. Here, you might be feeling one or more of these:

- Overwhelmed but stuck
- That there's lots of urgency, but it's impossible to do anything
- You need to do things, but you can't
- You must do all these things, but you don't know where to start
- Like you can't do anything
- Full of energy one minute and then exhausted the next

In this state of freeze stress response, you'll experience tonic immobility, which feels like you know you should do something, but your body completely freezes and you can't.

At times in life, you can move through the primary states; however, most of us have a home-from-home state that we spend most of our time in.

As an example, when I look at my own childhood, I was most definitely in my sympathetic nervous system for most of it, as my overachiever role always kept me fixing, solving problems and rescuing others to get love. But when there were times of extreme danger, my wonderful team of nervous-system ninjas would transport me into a dorsal ventral complex or freeze state, meaning I'd dissociate and disconnect so I didn't remember what was happening in the present.

This primary state carried over into my adult life. In my friendship group, I was called 'Super Mum' as I ran a business and worked long hours, but I never missed a play or football match my son was in; I became a master at juggling everything around to make sure I did everything. I still made time for my friends and social life, and when I'd then throw a relationship into the mix, I somehow also managed to take on managing my partner's life too. However, when I sensed danger, I went straight back into dorsal ventral complex and freeze modes, so I'd dissociate and disconnect again, and then run.

Now you understand more about what each state feels like, which one do you think is your primary home-from-home state?

♥ Ventral vagal complex

♥ Sympathetic nervous system

♥ Dorsal ventral complex

♥ Freeze

How your nervous-system state shows up in your relationships

When I understood more about my nervous system, I felt like it was such a light bulb moment in my life. It just made everything make sense, but what really blew my mind was how our nervous system and our attachment styles are intrinsically linked, and how that impacts our relationships.

Let's take a look at this.

In *Step 2*, we looked at how our early childhood experiences created the blueprint for how we show up in our relationships. If, for whatever reason, our primary caregivers were unable to meet our needs for consistent safety, love and connection, a secure attachment style was inhibited – meaning it wasn't available for us.

Let's say you had caregivers who were sometimes available for you and sometimes not. Your nervous system would have been saying, "I need your help, and you're not here. What should I do?"

Let's say you had caregivers who were sometimes dangerous and sometimes not. Your nervous system would have been saying, "I need your help as I don't feel safe. What should I do?"

Let's say you had caregivers who were sometimes calm and sometimes erratic. Your nervous system would have been saying, "I need help. I feel scared and don't know what to expect. What can I do?"

When your brilliant autonomic nervous system (and team of nervous-system ninjas) sees that your caregivers can't consistently meet your needs for safety, love and connection, then it jumps into action. It's saying, "Don't worry, little one; they might not be here for you consistently, but I am. I'm here, and I'm going to help you navigate through this so you can keep growing, you can keep developing and I can keep you safe."

Then your amazing self-protective system comes to your aid to help you remain safe. This totally blew my mind when I understood just how much our system is there for us and protecting us.

The way we attach to people is stored in our implicit experience or implicit memory. This means it's unconscious and automatic, and it's experienced through sensations, feelings and behaviours influenced by our autonomic nervous system. As an example, for some of you, when people get close to you, your body might slow down and get tense, or you might shut down around people; but when a person is distant, you might get anxious and need to move towards them. We use our autonomic nervous system in order to support us in our relationships.

Do you remember I said at the start of this step that understanding my autonomic nervous system was the missing link in my own healing? It's a missing link because it's impossible to get back in the driver's seat of your relationships without working with your nervous system, which is your sat nav that's directing you; it's not your conscious brain. If you've done loads of work on yourself, read every book, listened to every podcast and even been to therapy but you still find yourself repeating the same patterns, it's because you need to take some time to regulate your nervous system first so it understands it's safe to go in a new direction.

Regulating your nervous system is the key to everything because it influences how you relate to other people, how you set boundaries, and how you feel in relationships and life, and it holds the key to understanding how you react in relationships. When you find yourself experiencing difficulties, arguments or disconnections in your adult relationships, it's likely how you experienced difficulties in your childhood. So when difficulties happen, which they invariably will in relationships, your security guard (neuroception) googles previous experiences and what it did to protect you in the past, and it says, "Let's do that. Let's do the same thing now in your adult relationships." Then our autonomic nervous system comes to our aid.

This means you can do all of the inner work, but if you don't work on your nervous system, you'll continue in the same patterns and experience the same outcomes happening again and again in your relationships, because you can't read, learn or talk your way through to a secure attachment. You must regulate your way and feel your way into a secure attachment, working with your autonomic nervous system as a guide to help you get there.

When we were reviewing the different states earlier in this step, if you found you're mainly sympathetic-nervous-system dominant, then this often means you'll have an anxious attachment style, which can show up like this: "I feel safer when other people are close and less safe when I'm alone."

When difficulties arise in relationships, you may feel like you must fix it in order to be okay, so you go into your sympathetic nervous system. You think that, without fixing it, you won't be able to stay close to your partner, so you'll put all your focus on fixing and won't be able to focus on anything else. You may even disregard your own truth or your own needs at the expense of getting closeness again, because the system you learned as a child was this: "People aren't always available, but I need them and I don't feel safe alone, so I'm going to do everything I can in order to get love, connection and closeness."

If you found yourself to be more dorsal-vagal-system dominant in your nervous system, this often means you have an avoidant attachment style. This may show up in the form of connection or closeness feeling like a lot or overwhelming, so when someone comes towards you, you may feel like you just need to pull away, or you want to connect, but you just can't seem to.

Think of it like going to an island by yourself, as your system has learned to do that. You may have trouble asking for help, trouble with intimacy or trouble leaning on other people, which is the result of caregivers who weren't available for you or were dangerous for you. Your system learned this: "Let's go to this island and go alone, because that's the safe way."

If you've found yourself to be freeze dominant, this often means you have a disorganised attachment style. This can mean that you want people close to you, but as soon as someone is close, you either disappear or you push them away. But when they're far away, you want them close again; then when they're close, you push them away; when they're far away, you want them close again; and so it goes on.

When a difficulty arises, you may feel like you're in chaos and unsure whether you want that person close to you or far away; this is the result of caregivers who are sometimes dangerous and sometimes safe, so your system isn't entirely sure what to do.

It's important to note that, with nervous-system states and attachment styles, we can have a combination in given situations, but generally speaking, we usually have a predominant one.

If you've found you're ventral-vagal-system dominant, this often results in you having a secure attachment style, meaning you feel safe to be close to others and safe to be in relationships. When a difficulty arises, you know the relationship isn't over and it can be resolved once you're both feeling regulated.

The goal is having healthy and happy relationships, not draining, exhausting or out-of-control relationships where everything just feels like hard work. To achieve this goal, you have to master your nervous system as it's only then that you can change your attachment style and become more securely attached, which we're going to be looking at in the next step.

This step is absolutely imperative to healing and creating lasting change, but it's very often the step that many women forget to take; like me, they may previously have no idea just how much our nervous system and attachment style in relationships are intrinsically linked.

How your nervous-system state shows up in your health

Until I worked on my own nervous system, I also had no idea how much our nervous system affects our health.

Looking back, I was living in a chronic state of nervous-system dysregulation. The effects of living in this state included dissociation, being distracted, or feeling spacy or numb – hence my feeling of being so stuck. It also included confusion over what was happening and what was real; hyper vigilance or hyper arousal, and scanning for danger constantly; people-pleasing to avoid conflict or tension; and ignoring my own needs to put the needs of others first. All of these reactions were my body's way of saying, "I don't feel safe."

I wasn't aware that, when you've been living in this state for a prolonged period, you can enter what's called 'trauma body' or a chronic state of survival mode, which can then lead to even more effects on your body: exhaustion, insomnia, high emotional reactivity, feelings of dread, the inability to connect with others emotionally, living in fear and feeling out of control.

On top of having these emotional reactions, living in these dysregulated states for prolonged periods can also impact your physical health. There's now an incredible amount of research, including the work of Nicole Le Pera, the Holistic Psychologist,[12] to show that the brain and gut are in constant bi-directional communication with each other, so the brain can send signals to the gut, and the gut can send signals to the brain. The reason gut and brain health are so important is that 80% of our immune system is located in our gut, and to stay healthy, we need to have a healthy immune system, so it's ready when we need it to jump in – like our team of nervous-system ninjas – to get to the areas in our body where we need it most.

Your nervous system and gut health

So how does trauma effect the gut? This is a heavily researched area in science today; however, research (including that by Dr Gabor Maté)[13] has already proven that trauma has a direct impact on the gut, as the negative emotions and stress associated with trauma have a direct impact on our immune cells. Essentially, the more stress and negative emotions you have – which you'll have in a dysregulated state – the less effective your immune system becomes, potentially leading to chronic inflammation, which can further increase reactions such as extreme fatigue, insomnia, low mood, and lack of interest in yourself and your life.

When I discovered how our body stores unresolved trauma (through an incredible book called *The Body Keeps the Score* by Bessel Van Der Kolk)[14] and the link between gut health and nervous-system regulation (from the previously mentioned psychologist Nicole Le Pera),[15] it made complete sense why I developed chronic inflammation when I was with my ex and was later diagnosed with the inflammatory bowel disease ulcerative colitis.

Why are nervous-system regulation, the link between attachment styles and nervous-system regulation, and the link between gut health and nervous-system regulation so important?

They're important because you're reading this book to heal so you can have healthy and happy relationships, but you can't heal, change or implement anything you read if you're stuck in the dorsal ventral complex, too busy in the sympathetic-nervous-system state or experiencing tonic immobility in the freeze state. Living in a dysregulated nervous-system state also impacts how you relate to yourself and others, and it can prevent you having an emotional connection with others. Therefore, we need to understand how to regulate our nervous system, as having a regulated and healthy nervous system and a healthy gut are both part of the path to having healthier and happier relationships with yourself and others.

Take a moment to reflect on what you've discovered about your nervous system, then in the next step, we'll take a look at how you can regulate your nervous system.

Reflection exercise

"You can be a spectator in other people's lives or the conscious creator of your own."

– Fiona Challis

Step 7
Embodied & Somatic Healing

H A P P I N E S S

We've done the heavy lifting now, and hopefully, you're now beginning to understand why you've been experiencing issues in your relationships and why you've been feeling the way you have. Now it's time to start implementing everything you've learned and move towards getting you into a secure relationship with yourself and others, with a regulated nervous system and a healthy body – as, together, this is what's going to ignite you to act and to implement this, meaning this isn't just another book you've read. It's a book that's going to put you back in the driving seat so you're the conscious creator of your own life. In the final few steps, this is exactly what we're going to be doing, but first, let's summarise what you've discovered about yourself and your relationship blueprint so far, so we know where we're starting from.

Let's remind ourselves what we've learned so far and bring it all together so you can see what your relationship blueprint looks like.

If you've already completed these tasks, I recommend you do these again here, as seeing it in black and white will help you form a better picture of your current relationship blueprint.

In *Step 1*, we looked at the roles we may play as a young child to fit in, belong, and seek love and connection from our caregivers. What was the primary role you played?

The role I played was this:

- ♥ The carer

- ♥ The overachiever

- ♥ The sick one

- ♥ The difficult one

In *Step 2*, we considered how our earliest childhood experiences form our attachment style, which is how we relate to other people.

Which of the following four attachment styles was your primary one?

- ♥ Secure

- ♥ Anxious

- ♥ Avoidant

- ♥ Anxious–avoidant (fearful)

In *Step 3*, we thought about the beliefs that were contributing to our relationship programming. What limiting beliefs did you discover you were holding on to that were no longer serving you?

Complete these sentences:

I believed men were...

....

....

....

I believed love was...

....

....

....

I believed relationships were...

....

....

....

In *Step 4*, we also looked at how our beliefs, thoughts and feelings can form a protector part to keep us safe. What did you discover about the part that was in your life?

Complete these sentences:

The part that came into my life was…

....

....

Its job was to…

....

....

But I've now given it a new job to…

....

....

In *Step 5*, we met our inner child to understand how she felt as a child. What did you discover about your inner child?

Complete these sentences:

As a child, I felt…

....

....

As a child, I didn't feel...

....

....

As a child, I had...

....

....

As a child, I didn't have...

....

....

And that led me to believe...

....

....

In *Step 6*, we learned about the importance of our vagus nerve and how, when stressed within relationships, it sends us into one of four stress responses.

Which stress response did you feel you spent more time in?

- ♥ Fight

- ♥ Flight

- ♥ Fawn

- ♥ Freeze

We then looked at how, when we're confronted with a situation or person, our brilliant team of nervous-system ninjas jump in to protect us, and we learned about the primary states of regulation and dysregulation. Which state was your home-from-home state or the state you found yourself in the most?

- ♥ Ventral vagal complex (secure and regulated)

- ♥ Sympathetic nervous system (dysregulated, most likely with anxious attachment style)

- ♥ Dorsal ventral complex (dysregulated, most likely with avoidant attachment style)

- ♥ Freeze (dysregulated, most likely with an equal measure of anxious and avoidant attachment styles [fearful attachment style])

Looking back on your relationships to date, answer the following questions:

What percentage of time have you spent in each of the following states?

- • Regulated state ....
- • Dysregulated state ....

How has being in a dysregulated state impacted your relationships?

....

....

....

How has being in a dysregulated state impacted your emotional health?

....

....

....

How has being in a dysregulated state impacted your mental health?

....

....

....

How has being in a dysregulated state impacted your physical health?

....

....

....

How has being in a dysregulated state impacted your spiritual health?

....

....

....

All of this is incredible information to learn about yourself, and it will help start you on your healing journey and create lasting change, as to achieve both, we need to take an embodied approach to healing. Embodied healing is healing that goes beyond mental processing alone. Instead, it integrates the physical, mental, emotional and spiritual aspects of healing so you can finally be free from the things that have kept you from being your whole and authentic self in relationships.

This embodied healing must first begin with regulating your nervous system, as this is the key both to changing your relationship with yourself and others and to creating long and lasting change. For me, this was the missing link I'd been searching for and the thing that made the biggest difference to all the other work I'd done; this was because having a regulated nervous system in place meant all the other healing I'd done fell into place, like the pieces of a puzzle coming together.

Think of regulating your nervous system as being like laying the foundations of a house: when you have strong foundations in place, you can build a safe and solid new house, and all the bricks you lay slot perfectly together. The same applies to relationships, as a regulated nervous system lays the foundation to healthier and happier relationships.

Let's look at how we can each regulate our nervous system.

The first thing to do is to become aware of the state your autonomic nervous system is currently in, as it informs everything you experience about yourself and your relationships.

If you're in sympathetic nervous system, your feelings, behaviours, thoughts and the story you're telling yourself are going to match the traits of that state. Similarly, if you're in dorsal ventral complex or freeze, they're going to match the traits of the respective state. This, of course, means that if you're in regulation in ventral vagal complex, they're going to match that state's traits. So changing your state will then change your thoughts, behaviours, feelings and the story you tell yourself.

Tony Robbins, the world's most renowned motivational and life-transformation expert, has coined the phrase "Change your state, change your life", as that's how incredibly impactful your state can be, not just on your relationships but on your entire life.

By consistently being aware of your state, regulating your state and telling yourself a better story, you're also building up your database of positive experiences, so when your security guard – neuroception – does the equivalent of googling other similar experiences, you're providing more and more positive results, and eventually, when your positive experiences get to page one on your internal Google results equivalent, your autonomic nervous system starts to say, "I think this may be safe now," and when that happens, you can spend more and more time in the ventral vagal complex and regulated.

I've really simplified this teaching, as when I first started to study some of the neuroscience work behind polyvagal theory and somatic trauma work, I found it to be incredibly complex. By simplifying this, I hope you can see just how incredibly powerful you are in your own healing and that you have the power to heal your life and relationships, because you've always had the power inside you to regulate your nervous system. You have the power to get unstuck, and you have the power to have the healthy and happy relationships you deserve.

Regulating your nervous system allows you to be in control of your experience, rather than external circumstances having all the control, so you get back in the driver's seat and control your life, your relationships and your body. It will also support you in having overall happiness and a sense of belonging, connection and purpose, which we'll look at in the next step.

It allows you to make relationship choices in line with your truth, instead of making choices in line with a self-protective response; it allows you to enter relationships from a place of worth rather than old wounds. It can also help you physically as it brings your body into homoeostasis and can help to relieve many gut- or immune-system-based issues.

I honestly think nervous-system regulation is the best management medicine for our bodies. There's lots of research on this now, and not only that but – as someone who struggled with inflammatory bowel disease, spent a lot of my life dissociated and so disconnected from myself that I barely knew who I was any more, and was using every coping strategy under the sun to help me leave my body – I can honestly say from my own personal experience that everything changed when I focused on regulating my system and introduced somatic healing on top of the previous healing I'd already done. I found my health again, I found myself again and I completely changed my life, all so I could step towards my passion and purpose – something I'd struggled to do beforehand.

This is because we must *show*, not tell, our system that we're safe. When we can show it that we're safe again and again, it then begins to regulate, and this is what leads us to having the life and relationships we deserve.

Let's have a look at some regulating somatic exercises that will show your self-protective system you're safe and will explain how to talk to it in a language it understands.

The best exercise is to think of anything that registers as a good feeling for you and supports you to feel more present and grounded. Take a moment to think of an activity that does this for you.

However, be careful not to confuse coping strategies such as overworking, drinking, eating and shopping with regulating activities, as coping strategies help you to numb yourself and leave your body, whereas regulating exercises make you feel more present, grounded and in your body.

When I distinguished between both in my own journey, it was a light bulb moment for me: I realised it was no wonder that I felt so disconnected with myself, as I was using numbing activities not regulating activities. This was an important lesson for me as I realised that, to connect with others, I needed to be able to connect with myself first.

I honestly wish this were taught in schools, which I'm planning to start next year, as kids today are using so many coping strategies

– Xbox, gaming and social media to name a few – but these are all keeping them numb and stuck, rather than unstuck, connected and growing. I, for one, wish someone had taught me this when I was growing up.

There are two primary types of regulation exercises: self-regulation exercises, which are things you can do on your own to bring yourself into regulation and through the hierarchy of states until you reach your ventral-vagal-complex state; and there are co-regulation exercises you can do with other people.

Self-regulation exercises

Self-regulation exercises are things such as reading, meditating, being in nature, cooking, singing, listening to music, creating art or painting, spending time with animals, exercising, getting a massage, having acupuncture, dancing, going for a drive, humming, swaying, sitting in grass, being with a loved one or friend, playing games, writing (which is keeping me regulated right now), being in water, swimming, walking, listening to calming music, moving physically, or hiking. Which activities resonate with you the most and which do you enjoy the most?

If you've identified yourself as more anxiously attached, it's very beneficial to introduce more self-regulation exercises into your daily life, as by doing so, you're showing your nervous system that it's safe to be alone.

My favourite self-regulation exercises are walking and being by water. I'm fortunate enough to live by a beautiful river, and I walk alongside it every morning as it helps me to feel more grounded. I love being in nature, I mediate daily, I journal daily, I love dancing, and I love singing out loud when I go for a long drive.

Try making a list of three self-regulation exercises you can at least try this week to see if you like them:

The three self-regulation exercises I'll try are these:

1. ....
2. ....
3. ....

Co-regulation exercises

Co-regulation exercises are other regulation exercises that you can do with others. These co-regulation exercises work so well because connection with others brings us regulation. If you've identified yourself as more avoidantly attached, co-regulation exercises are great, as they teach your nervous system that it's safe to be around other people.

Examples of great co-regulation exercises include joining a support group or coaching group, going to church, being part of a choir, being part of a sports team, making plans with friends, joining a fitness class or yoga class, or being part of a mums group, if you have kids. This can also include watching a TV show, but be careful that you don't binge watch and slip into coping strategies rather than using it as a co-regulation exercise. If you remember, at the start of this book, I talked about how I used to love watching a TV show called *The Waltons*, and knowing what I know now, I believe watching that show was 60 minutes of co-regulation for me, as I always felt so good and happy watching it.

This is the amazing power of co-regulation, as we actually have something called 'mirror neurons' that enable our nervous systems to read one another. So, when I was watching *The Waltons*, and the characters' nervous systems were all so calm and regulated, my mirror neurons jumped into action and helped me to become more calm and regulated. This is an important lesson for relationships and everyone reading this book, because the opposite can also apply – this means that if you're primarily in a dysregulated state, you'll be attracting dysregulated partners, and two dysregulated people together can lead to a very unhealthy relationship.

Co-regulation can also happen just by being around others. As an example, you could be working in a coffee shop and, without even having to talk to the other people, you can still feel more regulated as their nervous systems can also regulate yours. When I was in the pray stage of my healing journey, I used to love joining masterclasses and going to seminars, as just by being around women who were also on a similar journey to me made me feel very connected and therefore regulated.

The best co-regulating experience I've ever had was at a Tony Robbins event called Unleash the Power Within, which I attended in London. The event was four days long, there were 13,000 people attending, and the energy within that room was something I've never experienced before: it felt like we were all one, that everyone was in complete sync with each other and each was in regulation with themself. On the first night, following a 11-hour day, Tony led us all outside the venue to do his famous fire walk and demonstrate to us just how much power we have over our minds and nervous-system regulation. Despite seeing burning, red-hot coals in front of us, we all walked over those coals and did the fire walk that evening, as for 11 hours beforehand, we'd been priming our subconscious minds and showing our systems that it was safe. If that doesn't prove just how much power we each have over ourself and our nervous system, I don't know what will!

Think about and write down some co-regulation exercises or activities that could help you on your journey towards regulation and a secure attachment style:

The co-regulation exercises I'll try are…

....

....

....

Some of my favourite co-regulation exercises are joining coaching programs or mastermind groups, which help me show my nervous system that I don't have to keep doing everything by myself and it's safe to trust other people and ask for help; working from coffee shops, as the background noise helps me to focus more; joining a fitness class or yoga class; and being with friends and family, as I love just laughing and being together.

Moving forwards after you've read this book, I'd love to encourage you include at least one self-regulation exercise daily, so you can begin to show your system it's safe to be alone, and at least one co-regulation exercise or activity weekly, which will really help you to regulate yourself and get connection.

I'd also highly recommend that you have regular check-ins with yourself throughout the day so you can consciously be aware of your state and where you're spending your time. As an example, I set an alarm on my phone to go off every couple of hours as I now know I was spending a lot of time in a sympathetic-nervous-system state and daydreaming of the future as a coping mechanism, so when my alarm goes off, I just check in with myself and ask, "Where am I right now? Am I focusing on the past, present or future? Which state am I in?" I'll then do a grounding activity, such as looking around me to see three things, sensing smells around me or identifying what I can hear around me, which is to bring myself back into the present moment. This very simple exercise saves me hours every week that I'd otherwise have spent daydreaming about the future.

All these exercises are great ways to show, not tell, your nervous system that you're safe.

Let's have a look at some more examples of embodied healing practices to show your system that it's safe.

Emotional regulation

As children, many of us weren't taught the value or practice of being emotionally aware; instead, many of us were told off as a kid, and we ultimately sent a signal to our nervous system that it wasn't safe to talk about our emotions, so our team of nervous-system ninjas then suppressed all our emotions.

Examples of how we were told off could be the following:

- "Stop crying!"
- "Don't be such a baby!"
- "Wipe your eyes and just get on with it."
- "Don't let your father seeing you crying, or…"
- "Stop whining!"
- "Be quiet!"
- "Grow up!"
- "Stop complaining!"
- "You're just too much!"

Ultimately, as children, when we didn't feel seen or heard or didn't have our emotions and feelings acknowledged, we began to think that nobody cared about our emotions and feelings, so we held them deep inside. However, feelings are there to be felt, and emotions are there to be expressed, so as the adult you are today, I'd highly recommend introducing some emotional-awareness exercises into your life.

This can be as simple as just asking yourself the following:

- What am I feeling right now?
- What emotions are coming up for me right now?
- Who made me feel this in the past?

And then you should allow yourself to feel the feelings and express your emotions through talking about them, witnessing what they feel like to you, noticing what caused the emotion to arise, and writing or journalling about your feelings and emotions.

I personally find journalling is a great way to show my nervous system that it's safe to talk about my emotions and feelings. Even when I'm out and I don't have my daily journal with me, I just use the notes app in my phone to express what I'm feeling or what emotions have come up, as something special happens when you actually write about it; it's like a form of release that acknowledges your thoughts and feelings, and in doing so, you help your system to regulate. Then you can ask your body what it needs from you to feel better.

This could be doing one of the following:

- Deep belly breaths to calm and assure you
- Sleep, if your body is telling you it's tired
- Having a cup of tea or something nice to eat, if your body is trying to tell you it's hungry

- Getting a hug from a friend or loved one, if your body wants connection and to feel safe
- Listening to some calming music, if your body is saying it needs to relax
- Dancing, singing or exercise, if your body is saying it needs to get mobile
- Any of the self-regulation or co-regulation exercises we talked about previously

The important thing is to let your feelings and emotions be seen and heard, and also to recognise that, as a child, you may not have had this luxury, but as the adult you are today, you do have this luxury as you have complete control over making your feelings and emotions seen, heard and experienced, and you have complete control over regulating your nervous system – you just need to make time for yourself to do it.

The following is an incredibly powerful teaching I've received from my mentor Marissa Peer during the last three years, which I'd love to pass on and share with you, as it's a compelling reminder of just how important it is to feel our feelings and express our emotions:

"The feeling that cannot find it's expression in tears may cause other organs to weep." – Marisa Peer

This resonated with me so much at the time I got this teaching, as I was still coming to terms with the break-up with Seamus. I felt lied to, used and stupid for believing in him when I should have seen the signs. I wasn't talking about my feelings or emotions a lot as I felt ashamed and full of guilt. On top of this, I then suffered a major blow when I was betrayed by a family member, and this threw me straight back into my old habits of stuffing my feelings down, feeing like nobody cared and my feelings didn't matter, and no one was listening anyway, so why should I talk about them and express them? Shortly afterwards, I was diagnosed with an inflammatory bowel disease called ulcerative colitis, and I was admitted to hospital with chronic inflammation.

Later, when I learned more about the link between our brain and gut, and about the interconnection between polyvagal theory and somatic healing, my condition made perfect sense. I wasn't expressing my emotions, I wasn't feeling my feelings, and I wasn't aware of or listening to what my body was trying to tell me, so it had found a way to weep.

Through being more present and having a daily emotional-regulation practice, I was able to get the condition under control. I was later able to come off all the steroid medications when I learned something called the Wim Hof Method, which is based on breathing exercises, commitment to self, and controlled exposure to cold through having ice baths or a daily cold shower – which is what I do each day – to influence my body's immune system consciously and reduce naturally the inflammation I had.

It's no exaggeration to say that every client who contacts me to support them through joining my embodied therapy and coaching programs has a dysregulated nervous system, and many also suffer from poor gut health or immune-system-based illnesses, which is why taking an embodied approach to your healing is even more important and also why having a healthy and happy relationship with yourself – at physical, mental, emotional and spiritual levels – needs to be your first priority. Without feeling fully connected, cherished and loved by yourself, you can't be fully connected, cherished and loved by others.

In the next step, we'll look at more ways in which you can further build a deep connection with yourself on all levels, but in the meantime, before you start the next step, I'd encourage you to review all the work you've done so far to heal. And if you haven't already worked on regulating your nervous system, then make a promise to yourself to introduce at least one self-regulation and one co-regulation exercise to your life, as this is going to be the foundation that will facilitate you having healthy and happy relationships with yourself and others.

If you haven't already made a list, make it now:

1. ....

2. ....

3. ....

4. ....

5. ....

"Most people are only as needy as their unmet needs."

– Dr Amir Levine

Step 8
Secure Self

In the previous steps, we've reviewed your past to understand more about where and how your relationship blueprint has developed over time. This is an important first step to take, as you can't change what you don't understand. Next, we looked at how to become more present by bringing your inner child into your life today so you can reparent her to keep her feeling safe and heard, and then we studied how to regulate your nervous system, so you can show it that it's safe to heal and move forward in your relationships and your life.

In this step, we'll look at the future, as we're going to begin to design the life you want and the relationships you want to have in your life, and we'll rewrite your relationship blueprint so you can have secure, healthy and happy relationships with yourself and others.

The place to start is by having a healthy and happy relationship with yourself, which is where having a secure future relationship begins. Having a secure relationship with yourself means healing and letting go of your wounds from the past, so you can then step into your future secure self and relationships – whether that's a new relationship or within your existing relationship – with a clean slate and from a place of worth not wounds.

Letting go of wounds – such as releasing unresolved trauma, hurt, resentment, anger or anything else you feel is keeping you chained to the past – is best done with a licensed therapist, coach or practitioner, as they're trained to be an empathic witness and to hold a safe place for you to express your feelings and be seen and heard without judgement, which then shows, not tells, your nervous system that it's safe to let go now. However, there are some interventions you can begin to do yourself. The first is a positive-psychology intervention called a 'forgiveness letter'.

For many, forgiveness is one of the most difficult practices, but it can also be one of the most rewarding as it's one of the best gifts you can give yourself. When you forgive, you are relieved of the heavy burden of resentment you've been carrying, which has been weighing your relationships down. You become lighter in your spirit, and things in your life and relationships begin to fall into place.

In saying that, as someone who's experienced a lot of trauma during my childhood, I know very well that the struggle to forgive yourself and the people in your life who've hurt you is real and it's painful. But know this: it's not about condoning whatever the person did to mistreat you, rather it's about allowing what they did *not* to affect your life and relationships negatively today.

Dr Gerald Jampolsky, an internationally recognised authority in the field of psychiatry and the author of *Forgiveness: The Greatest Healer of All*, put it best when he said in an interview with Oprah Winfrey, "Forgiveness is giving up the hope that the past could have been any different."[16]

Forgiveness is accepting the reality of what did happen and moving on. This truth has been fundamental to allowing me to live my best life, and it has transformed my relationships with myself and with others.

It's easy to hear, and I understand it's harder to do, but the key is to sit with the hurt and feel it to then let go of it, otherwise it will keep popping up in your life, as it's being suppressed rather than acknowledged. It's uncomfortable, but when you can rise up, just meet that pain face to face and then let it flow through you, only then can you let it go and step out of the hurt of your history into the possibility of the present.

In the previous step, we talked about the importance of embodied healing and healing at emotional, mental, physical and spiritual levels; forgiveness is how you heal at a spiritual level. For some time, I've carried with me this lesson from Iyanla Vanzant, international speaker and spiritual leader.

I remember years ago she said this:

"You can accept or reject the way you're treated by other people. But until you heal the wounds of your past, you'll continue to bleed. You can bandage the bleeding with food, with alcohol, with drugs, with work, with cigarettes, with sex. But eventually it's going to ooze through and stain your life. You must find the strength to open up the wounds, stick your hands inside, pull out the core of the pain that is holding you in your past—the memories—and make peace with them." [17]

Let's take the steps to meet secure you by accepting what has happened, accepting the now, forgiving yourself, forgiving others, and giving up the hope that the past could have been anything other than what it was – as that's the secret to healing and becoming your secure self.

The self-forgiveness letter

Often, when we think about forgiveness, we only think about forgiving others who've wronged us in some way. But what about forgiving ourselves? What about forgiving ourselves instead of beating ourselves up for our past relationship choices and behaviours that we now know were made through the eyes of a hurt inner child? What about forgiving ourselves for how we reacted in certain situations, now we know it was our protector parts and team of nervous-system ninjas simply trying to protect us from what they still perceived as danger? What about forgiving ourselves and releasing any feelings of shame, guilt, resentment and anger we have towards ourselves? This exercise will help you write a letter of forgiveness to yourself.

To start with, think of a relationship, time or event in your life that you now recognise you'd like to let go of, and then answer the following questions:

What is it specifically about this relationship, time or event that you've been holding on to?

....

....

....

What feelings arise for you when you think about this event?

....

....

....

If you could go back in time, knowing what you know now, how would you have reacted or behaved differently?

....

....

....

As the informed adult you are today, what would you like to say to your old self about how you reacted or behaved?

....

....

....

If you feel it was your inner child, protector parts or nervous system that was showing up to protect you because it perceived danger within this relationship, what would you say to your inner child, protector parts or nervous system now you're looking back through a more informed lens?

....

....

....

Taking all this into consideration, what would you like to forgive yourself for?

....

....

....

What will you differently next time as a result of your newfound learning?

....
....
....

To finish, please complete the following sentences:

I forgive myself for...

....
....
....

I release any feelings of...

....
....
....

I now know more, and when I'm faced with a similar situation again, I'll...

....
....
....

And just let it go. It's like the water in the shower: once it's gone, you can't take it back.

The forgiveness letter for others

The next people for you to forgive are those who hurt you, but please be aware that this is completely a personal choice to make, and it's always very heavily dependent on what happened, so if you don't feel comfortable doing this part, that's fine, simply wait until you're ready or focus on the forgiveness letter you've already written to yourself, which is most important letter of all.

If you're ready, you can start by thinking of someone in your life – past or present – who's caused you suffering, whom you resent and whom you'd like to forgive, then follow the next prompts to help you write your forgiveness letter.

It's important to note that you're writing this letter for yourself. You aren't writing it for them, and you aren't going to be sending it to them. You're writing this letter to acknowledge the pain deep at your core that this person caused you, so you can then pull it out, let it go and make peace with it.

Write your forgiveness letter on a **separate sheet of paper**, and remember that there's no right or wrong here; just let it flow.

Afterwards, I suggest you throw the letter away, so that you're no longer holding on to it.

Follow these prompts [the words in square brackets are instructions to you and the words in italics are what you should write]:

[Write their name],

You really hurt me when... [tell them how they hurt you].

And that made me feel... [tell them how you felt].

[Acknowledge the feelings that are coming up for you and where those feelings are being experienced in your body.]

It made me believe that I... [tell them the beliefs you formed about yourself because of this hurt].

[Then write the following:]

But I don't need those beliefs any more because that's not me any more.

It's not me now because I'm ... [write your age] *years old now.*

It's not me because...[Tell them why it's no longer you. You may give several reasons; for example, because you're an adult now, you're independent, you have a job or business, you have your own home, you have more self-confidence, you know the difference between right and wrong, you're educated, or you know more.]

[Then write the following:]

What you did was... [write a word/phrase here that sums up what you think about what happened; for example, "What you did

165

was wrong."], *but it happened, it's now in the past where it belongs, and so are you.*

I'm now releasing any hurt and I'm releasing you, as I'll no longer allow you or what happened to impact my life and relationships.

I forgive you and release you for my own benefit, as I deserve to be... [write what you feel you deserve].

Because, today, I'm choosing me, I'm taking my power back, and I know I'm in full control of my life, my mind and my body.

Best wishes,

[Sign your name]

Now you've written your letter, I want you to imagine those feelings, identify where you felt them in your body, and then see them leaving your body and floating away until you can only see them far in the past behind you.

Congratulations, my dear, and well done on taking the courageous step to forgive, as on the other side of forgiveness is freedom. The freedom to live the life for which you were intended – and the one you actually deserve. The freedom to have the healthy and happy relationship you deserve to have with yourself and others.

Now let's start to create what your new life and relationships will look like.

Meet your secure self

In *Step 5*, we looked at the story of the golden Buddha and how layers of clay can form on us over the years until we lose all sight of the gold that sits within us. The same can happen in relationships where, over time, you've become so accustomed to putting others' needs first, people-pleasing, ignoring your own needs and developing learned behaviours on how to seek love and connection; however, all these take us so far away from our own gold and our authentic self that many of us women feel like we've lost ourselves in relationships or we don't know who we are or what we like any more. We crave having an authentic relationship with others, but we don't know how to have an authentic relationship with ourselves, as we rarely sit down to ask ourselves the right questions so we can really get to know ourselves again and get in touch with who we really are and what we like.

Let's start by you spending some time answering a few of these questions so you can become more secure in expressing what *you* want, like, need and value, and what makes you happy. Write your answers below:

What do you want?

....

....

....

What do you like?

....
....
....

What do you need?

....
....
....

What makes you happy?

....
....
....

Next, we'll create what your best-possible secure future self looks like using a positive-psychology intervention called 'your best-possible self'.

'Best-possible secure self' exercise

For this exercise, I'd like you to go somewhere quiet with no distractions. Set a timer for about 10–15 minutes, during which time you'll close your eyes and visualise your best-possible secure self. Then I'd like you to imagine the following:

- Your life and relationships are going exactly how you'd like them to go in the future and everything has turned out as you desired.

- You've accomplished your goals of feeling secure in yourself and your life dreams, and you're living your best-possible secure life.

- You've found your self-confidence, self-esteem and self-worth, and you feel incredibly secure in yourself.

To get the most out of this exercise, make it about *you* – not about anyone else.

When you've completed this visualisation of your best-possible secure self in your mind, spend around 20 minutes journalling your best-possible future. Don't worry about it being perfect, just use this exercise as an opportunity to express what was in your heart during your visualisation. Here are a few prompts to help you get started:

- What was your secure self doing?

- What was secure you thinking?

- What was secure you saying to yourself?

- How did you look and dress?

- How did secure you feel within yourself?

Take some time to really get in touch with your secure self. Make a note of what came up for you on the next page.

My best-possible secure self

Reflection from your feelings

After completing the initial exercise, reflect on your feelings. Some questions to think about are:

- What effects did this exercise have?
- How did this exercise affect you emotionally?
- How did this exercise affect your current self-image?
- Did this exercise motivate or inspire you?
- How did this exercise affect you overall?
- How did this exercise open you up to possibilities?

I'd like you take a moment to think about being your secure self again, and then circle the statement out of the following that resonates with you the most about the reality of becoming the secure self you've seen in your visualisation.

- ♥ I'll believe it when I see it.

- ♥ I'll see it when I believe it.

The statement that will help you manifest and bring secure you to life is "I'll see it when I believe it", because when you believe in yourself, you can reclaim your life and fulfil your dreams of becoming secure, so you can have healthy, happy and loving relationships with yourself and others. For this reason, I'd encourage you to spend 5–10 minutes daily doing this exercise to feel those feelings and think those thoughts that secure you had in your visualisation, as that's what will uncover your gold and make your thoughts a reality.

Your values and what's important to you

Understanding your values, especially when it comes to relationships, is incredibly important because a relationship where you each have completely opposing values can become very unhealthy, whereas a relationship in which the values of both of you are aligned is much healthier and therefore much happier.

So what are values? Values are what make you feel aligned; they're like your internal compass, which helps to keep you on your path and identify when you're steering off it. Your values guide how you think, feel and behave, and your values give your life meaning and purpose.

If you've ever met someone or witnessed a situation where you had a strong feeling that something didn't feel right about them, that's your values in action.

Research by Christopher Peterson, Martin Seligman and VIA[18] has shown that we experience higher levels of well-being overall when we're aligned to our values, and we feel good, but when we aren't aligned to our values, we feel bad. Likewise, in relationships, when you live in accordance with your values and make choices in line with them, you'll have higher levels of alignment and well-being in your relationships. Many of the women I work with – especially those who, in the past, have been busy looking after everyone else's needs but neglecting theirs – find this exercise difficult, as they can't remember the last time anyone even asked how they were, never mind what their values are. If this is you, please don't worry, as I'm going to help you to identify your values in this section.

To identify your values, I'd like you to think of a time when everything was working in your life and relationships, and you were feeling really good. If you can't think of such a time, you can also use the visualisation of your best-possible future secure self and what made you feel really good in that.

Now I'd like to you look at the following list of values and circle what stands out for you or feels like you. Don't think about it too much – just trust your instinct to circle those values that resonate most with you.

- ♥ Authenticity
- ♥ Adventurousness
- ♥ Fairness
- ♥ Love
- ♥ Optimism
- ♥ Positivity
- ♥ Connection to others
- ♥ Balance
- ♥ Accountability
- ♥ Reliability
- ♥ Contribution
- ♥ Inspiring others

- ♥ Courage
- ♥ Honesty
- ♥ Creativity
- ♥ Loyalty
- ♥ Freedom
- ♥ Family
- ♥ Integrity
- ♥ Joy
- ♥ Humility
- ♥ Respect
- ♥ Well-being
- ♥ Learning

- ♥ Wealth
- ♥ Leadership
- ♥ Success
- ♥ Openness
- ♥ Empathy
- ♥ Kindness
- ♥ Justice
- ♥ Humour

- ♥ Hope
- ♥ Growth
- ♥ Appreciation of beauty
- ♥ Friendship
- ♥ Peace
- ♥ Gratitude
- ♥ Spirituality
- ♥ Good judgement

Next, think about who you admire; in particular, what are the qualities you admire about them? What does that tell you about what you value?

....

....

....

Also answer the following questions:

Looking at the future, when the secure you shows up in relationships, which values do you want to show up with?

....

....

....

What values would you like your partner to have or what values would you like to see in your current relationship?

....

....

....

How are the values that you and your partner are showing up with aligned?

....

....

....

On a scale of 1–10, with 10 being 'strongly agree' and 1 being 'strongly disagree', how would rate your score in terms of your partners showing up with the values you admire the most?

....

When your time on this planet comes to an end, what would you like to be remembered for?

....

....

....

Who do you want to be when you are healed, happy and living in-line with your values?

....

....

....

When I completed this values exercise on my own healing journey, I found it very powerful as, first, I couldn't remember the last time I actually took some time out to think about me and what I wanted as my life, and relationships were more like a roller coaster than a reflection period. Second, I realised just how much my relationships and my life were out of alignment with my core values, which explained why they always felt like such hard work.

My top 10 core values are these:

1. Empathy
2. Inspiring others
3. Positivity
4. Relating to others
5. Learning
6. Appreciating beauty and excellence
7. Leadership
8. Kindness
9. Gratitude
10. Social intelligence

Comprehending your values helps you to understand yourself better, and when you do that, you not only understand your wants and needs better but it also helps you to express your needs better in relationships and back them up with the scientific research that sits behind them.

There are lots of free online tools that can also help you to identify your core values, and I'd also recommend the VIA survey (**www.viacharacter.org/survey/account/register**), which you may find easier. This online survey is free to take; however, I'd also recommend that you purchase the comprehensive report to get a deeper understanding of how your core values show up for you.

Now that you're beginning to learn a little more about yourself and what you value, our next step is to understand how you like to be loved.

Identifying your love language

Lastly, I'd like to spend some time helping you to identify your preferred love language, which is key to helping you feel more loved, seen and heard in your relationships.

Not everyone gives love in the same way, and likewise, people have different ways they prefer to receive love. The concept of love languages was developed by Gary Chapman in his book *The 5 Love Languages: The secret to love that lasts*, where he describes five unique styles of communicating love (both giving and receiving), having distilled these categories from his experience in marriage counselling and linguistics: *words of affirmation, quality time, receiving gifts, acts of service* and *physical touch*.[19]

We may all relate to most of these languages, but each of us has one that speaks to us the most. Discovering your partner's and your primary love language and speaking that language regularly can lead to having a better understanding of each other's needs and supporting each other's growth, which leads to having a healthier and happier relationship.

Here's an overview of each of the five love languages.

Words of affirmation

People whose love language is words of affirmation value verbal acknowledgement of affection, including frequently hearing, "I love you," compliments, words of appreciation, verbal encouragement and, often, frequent digital communication, such as texting and social media engagement. These words of affirmation make us feel understood and appreciated.

Quality time

People whose love language is quality time feel the most adored when their partner actively wants to spend time with them. They particularly love it when active listening, eye contact and full presence are prioritised hallmarks in the relationship. This love language is all about getting your partner's undivided attention, without the distraction of TV, phone screens or any other outside interference.

Acts of service

If your love language is acts of service, you value when your partner goes out of their way to make your life easier. It's things such as bringing you soup when you're sick, making your coffee for you in the morning, taking the bins out, or picking up your dry cleaning for you when you've had a busy day at work. This love language is for people who believe that actions speak louder than words. Unlike those who prefer to hear how much they're cared for, people who prefer this love language like to be *shown* they're appreciated.

Gifts

Gifts is a straightforward love language: you feel loved when people give you 'visual symbols of love', otherwise known as gifts. It's not about the monetary value, but rather the symbolic thought behind the item. People with this love-language style recognise and value the gift-giving process: the careful reflection, the deliberate choosing of the object to represent the relationship, and the emotional benefits from receiving the present. People whose love language is receiving gifts enjoy being given something that's both physical and meaningful.

Physical touch

People with physical touch as their love language feel loved when they receive physical signs of affection, including kissing, holding hands, cuddling on the couch and sex. Physical intimacy and touch can be incredibly affirming and serve as a powerful emotional connector for people with this love language. The roots of this can often go back to someone's childhood because some people only felt deep affection and love from their parents when they were held, kissed or hugged.

How finding my love language helped me:

I absolutely loved finding out about my order of preference of love languages, which came out as this:

- Acts of service (37%)
- Words of affirmation (23%)
- Quality time (20%)
- Physical touch (10%)
- Receiving gifts (10%)

It helped me to realise why a partner cooking dinner or running a bath for me when I was busy meant more to me than him buying me an expensive gift.

Love-language quiz

To find out your love language, visit the book resources page where I've provided access to a really good free online quiz: **www.rapidrelationshiptherapy.com/bookresources**.

Summary

Wow! In this step, you've forgiven and let go, you've met your best-possible secure self, and you've identified your values and your preferred love language. That's incredible progress for you to make, so before moving on to the final step, let's just take some time to reflect on what you've discovered about yourself and to regulate your system.

Before we move on to the next step, take a few moments to either write down (if you prefer to self-regulate) or to tell someone (if you prefer to co-regulate) three things you've discovered about your values and your love language and how they'll help you to become secure and have happy and healthy relationships with yourself and others. (Ideally, get your partner to identify their values and love language too.)

Reflection exercise

"To love oneself is the beginning of
a lifelong romance."

– Oscar Wilde

Step 9
Self-love

We've now reached the final phase of my healing journey: the self-love phase in which my true transformation happened. Before starting this journey, when I thought of self-love, I thought of having a lovely bubble bath, listening to my favourite music or taking time relax after a hard day at work, but I now realise that true self-love is much more than that. Before we look at what true self-love involves, let me first dispel a very common myth that some women I work with believe about self-love.

Does focusing on yourself and self-love make you a narcissist?

Like me, many women I work with have unfortunately experienced being in a relationship with a narcissist, whom we know from the previous step are very self-focused people. Bearing this in mind, a common misconception many women have is that self-love and putting yourself and your needs first are narcissistic traits, so let me explain the difference between having self-love and being a narcissist. Simply put, a narcissist doesn't have self-love. They're typically men who are very confident externally, but internally, they have incredibly low self-esteem, low self-worth and no self-love. They also have no self-awareness as they're truly certain of the stories and the beliefs they tell themselves, despite most of them being completely delusional.

So, does having self-awareness and having disciplined self-love practices to increase your self-esteem and self-worth make you a narcissist? Absolutely not! In fact, it's quite the opposite, as having self-love is a healthy practice, and it's the key to attracting and keeping a secure, healthy, happy and loving relationship.

True self-love

True self-love comprises of six aspects – self-acceptance, self-worth, self-esteem, self-care, setting boundaries and self-discipline – all of which require time, effort, energy and attention to cultivate.

Self-love is the practice of treating yourself with kindness, compassion and love. Just as you'd give a loved one your time, understanding and respect, truly engaging in self-love requires the same. Loving oneself is a powerful thing to do, but it can often prove difficult, especially for women who didn't witness self-love from their caregivers growing up. If you're one such woman, perhaps you witnessed your parents being harsh or critical to themselves or others, and in turn, you became your own worst critic and you judge yourself more harshly than you would another person whose inner life you can't see.

Part of self-love is recognising this, as the first step to having true self-love is having self-awareness and accepting that your first experience of it may not be the level of self-love you need today, recognising and accepting that this didn't start with you, and unlearning and relearning belief patterns and programs that have kept you stuck in the past – which is exactly what you've been doing whilst reading this book, so your journey to self-love has already begun.

Self-acceptance

Self-acceptance is understanding and accepting the parts of yourself you think need to be changed right alongside accepting the things you like about yourself. It's about acknowledging those parts you want to change with an 'and that's okay' attitude, instead of looking at yourself and speaking to yourself with judgement and condemnation. It boils down to loving all of yourself, not just part of yourself (mind, body and spirit) the way you'd want others to love you.

To cultivate more self-awareness, you can start to become more conscious of your thoughts, how they affect your emotions and how your emotions then cause you to act. You can become more aware of what makes you feel sad or angry and what makes you act impulsively, and then just acknowledge and witness the feelings, so you can then become more mindful. The same applies to what and whom makes you happy; you should become more aware of this, and then take the time to recognise and sit in the feeling of happiness when it occurs.

Self-acceptance is giving yourself space to examine your thoughts, feelings and actions, and when you become more cognisant of them, you can do more of what makes you happy, and also avoid or say no to people or situations that trigger negative thoughts, feelings and emotions in you.

A simple daily practice I use is just asking myself, "How does this person or this situation make me feel?" You could perhaps try asking yourself this question and see what answer comes up for you.

Self-worth

Self-worth is the belief we each have about ourself, and as we discovered in *Step 3*, these beliefs can often be limiting beliefs that we've carried through from our childhood, but they're a set of outdated beliefs that no longer serve us. Self-worth is recognising this and taking the time to turn those beliefs around into more empowering beliefs; it's about allowing yourself to remove the clay that has surrounded you, so you can uncover your true inner gold again. Self-worth lies in you coming home to yourself and in recognising all the great things about you – and you do have lots of great things about you! You've already practised increasing your self-worth by reading this book and letting go of those old beliefs that no longer serve you, so to continue practising improving your self-worth, try taking the time every day to recognise one amazing thing you like about yourself or one thing you feel you did right, and then you'll slowly begin to see over time just how awesome you are.

Self-esteem

Self-esteem results from self-worth. Having a high sense of self-worth results in high self-esteem. Self-worth is the realisation that you're awesome just as you are, despite what has or hasn't happened in your life and relationships. Having self-esteem is looking at yourself and saying, "Bloody hell, I've been through a lot, but my qualities of being able to bounce back, determination, and love for my family and friends got me through it, and I'm still here today and ready to let go and let love in again." When you develop a sense of self-worth, self-esteem will come more naturally.

When I work with children, I love doing fun exercises with them to help them increase their self-esteem and self-worth, because they learn better through play. One of the exercises I do is to give them a £50 note, along with bottles of ketchup, mayonnaise, sugar, salt and anything else they can find. I tell them to put the £50 note on the floor and throw everything we've found on top of it until it becomes really dirty and smelly. Then I ask them all to stamp on the £50 and say mean things to it, such as, "You're smelly," "You're no good," or, "You're worthless." They have great fun doing this exercise, and I have great fun watching them.

At the end of the exercise, I hold up a clean £50 note in one hand and the beaten-up and trodden on £50 note in the other hand, and then I ask them, "Which £50 note is worth more?" Generally, half of them will say the clean one, but the other half will always say the trodden-on £50 note. When I ask them why that is, they say it's because that one has more character or that one has been through more, which is so beautiful to see and hear from children at such a young age as it serves as a reminder that, no matter what happens to them, if someone calls them a name or says they don't like them, they have more character and they're worth more than anyone who feels they need to stamp all over other people to make themselves feel better.

To increase your self-esteem and self-worth, I'd encourage you to take hold of the same reminder, as you aren't broken, you're beautiful, you're lovable, you're enough and you're worth more now than you've ever been, as you're taking the time to embrace what was and create what are going to be healthy and happy relationships with yourself and others.

We accept the love we think we deserve, so increasing your self-worth and self-esteem and consciously taking some time every day to work on yourself will also help you to stick to the boundaries we're just about to complete.

Self-care

Self-care is all the acts we do to keep ourselves healthy, such as exercising, taking a bubble bath or shower, eating a balanced diet, staying hydrated and doing things we love. Self-care can also take the form of watching what you consume, such as the music you listen to, the things you watch and the people you spend time with. Compared to the other aspects of self-love, self-care is easier to do.

Here are some great self-care tips to get you started.

Physical exercise

I'm sure you already know that exercise is great for your physical health and body, but did you know it can also improve your mental health?

By exercising regularly, you'll get an enormous sense of well-being. You'll feel more energetic throughout the day, sleep better at night, and feel more relaxed and positive about yourself. Regular exercise can also have a profoundly positive impact on depression and anxiety, because it relieves stress, improves your self-esteem and self-worth, and can help you overcome previous trauma.

You don't have to be a fitness fanatic to reap the benefits. In fact, research by Lawrence Robinson, Jeanne Segal and Melinda Smith indicates that even modest amounts of exercise can make a real difference,[20] so think about what exercise you can implement in your daily routines. I'm not a huge gym fan, but I do love walking and being in nature, so my day always starts with taking a walk by the river, as it gets my body moving and my mind into a positive state for the day ahead.

Another reason I love walking is because there's now more and more evidence[21] to show that exercises that involve cross movement and that engage both arms and legs – such as walking – can actually help our nervous system become 'unstuck' and begin to move out of the freeze stress response we talked about in *Step 6*. Instead of letting my mind wander when I walk, I now focus on my body and how it feels when I walk; I pay close attention to the physical sensations in my joints and muscles, and by doing so, I feel more connected to my body again, which is incredibly important for me, considering how much I previously dissociated and felt disconnected. This means I start my day by self-regulating my nervous system.

If you don't like walking, you can also try running, swimming, weight training or dancing – that is, any exercise that gets both your arms and legs moving together.

Cultivate mindfulness

Positive psychology has found links between mindfulness and a range of positive outcomes, including healthy self-esteem. Cultivating mindfulness can be done through having a regular meditation practice. Even 10–15 minutes per day of focusing on your breathing in a quiet space and developing an awareness of your thoughts can put you on the right track. After some practice, you may find you're able to keep a more balanced perspective on things, including your view of yourself. If you're unsure how to mediate, there are tons of great apps such as Calm and Insight Timer, which I'd highly recommend.

Speak positively to yourself

Self-talk, or the way you speak to yourself privately and internally, can be powerful. Positive-psychology research has found that negative self-talk can be linked to depression and anxiety.[22] Most people wouldn't criticise and tear down someone they love so harshly, so why do we sometimes do it to ourselves? It's easy to slip into these negative thought patterns, but with practice, it's possible to alter them. It's likely to be worth the effort too, since positive self-talk is linked to higher levels of self-esteem, calmness and motivation.

A great practice to introduce when you find your inner chatter or inner critic taking over is to remind yourself that you aren't your thoughts, then take time to listen to what you're saying and ask yourself these questions:

- Would I speak to a young child (your inner child) the way I'm speaking to myself?
- How would someone who loves themselves speak to themselves?

Then reframe what you're saying in a positive light. This takes time to practice, but be compassionate with yourself and give yourself time, as it's likely you've been saying harsh, critical words to yourself for many years, and just like it takes a baby many attempts to walk, it will take you many attempts to practise positive self-talk, so just give yourself time and be kind to yourself.

Keep a gratitude journal

There's now a mounding pile of research (including an article by Tiffany Sauber Millacci)[23] that shows people who practise gratefulness are happier, have higher self-esteem and higher self-worth. By simply thinking daily about three things you're grateful for, you'll increase your overall happiness.

Let's give it a try by listing three things you are grateful for today:

1. ....

2. ....

3. ....

Keeping a gratitude journal is a non-negotiable for me. I start my day by writing everything I'm grateful for and I end my day by writing three things I've been grateful for during my day. By doing this, I start and end my day well, and I'd highly encourage you to do the same, as it really does have an incredibly powerful and positive impact on your overall well-being.

Writing rainy-day notes

Writing rainy-days notes is something I learned from Lewis Howes in his brilliant podcast series *The School Of Greatness*,[24] and they've helped me immensely. The concept is to write yourself a note anytime you achieve something you're proud of, or to write one about any obstacles or challenges you've overcome in life, and then, when you get one of those rainy days in life where everything feels impossible, you read your rainy-day notes to remind yourself just how much you've achieved.

Let's give it a try today by listing three things you've already overcome in your life that you're proud of:

1. ....
2. ....
3. ....

Reading rainy-day notes brings sunshine to every rainy day.

Learning to say no – saying no to others is saying yes to yourself

True self-care and self-love are putting your needs first. It isn't selfish; it's a necessity, as without looking after yourself and your own needs, you can end up over-giving and being the fixer of everything, and you'll eventually burn out.

A good practice when it comes to saying no or not jumping in to to fix something is simply asking yourself some check-in questions such as these:

- Is it my job to fix this?
- Did they ask me to fix this?
- Who am I doing this for? For me or to please someone else?

If you're genuinely doing it for yourself, and it's adding to your self-care, then you're making the right choice; however, if you're doing it for others, and it's not your job to fix or please them, then you're neglecting yourself.

If you find yourself people-pleasing, always saying yes and neglecting your own needs to make others happy, a great practice to introduce is a weekly reflection practice that I was first introduced to by Gabor Maté in his incredible book *The Body Says No*.[25] This weekly reflection practice is where you ask yourself the following questions at the end of each week:

Where did I not say no this week where I should have, but I felt I couldn't as I was people-pleasing or worried about what others would think of me if I said no?

....

....

....

What was the impact to me personally of not saying no?

....

....

....

What did I believe consciously or subconsciously would happen if I said no?

....

....

....

If I said no, then... [complete the sentence]

....

....

....

Who would I be if I knew how to say no?

....

....

....

Where is it in my life that I'm not saying yes to myself?

....

....

....

Try repeating this exercise for the next few weeks so you can start to see how often you're saying no to yourself.

Practising self-care in ways like this is putting yourself first. When it's done in a way that's right for you, taking good care of yourself can be a huge contributor to your self-love journey.

Setting boundaries

Setting boundaries is an act of self-love and a way you can increase your sense of self-worth in relationships, as by setting boundaries, you're saying you know you're worth it, and you aren't afraid to make sacrifices to maintain your own health and happiness and to ensure your needs are also met.

Unfortunately, many women who come to me for support have little or no boundaries in place because they were always putting the needs of others first, people-pleasing and ignoring their own needs; some have no idea what their needs are, and therefore they have no boundaries set around those needs.

Think of boundaries as the fence around your garden to separate it from your neighbours' gardens. In relationships, boundaries are clear limits that separate you – in terms of your needs, wants, thoughts, beliefs, emotions, and physical and emotional space – from others; they're necessary for you to develop and maintain authentic relationships.

A lack of boundaries in childhood often results in a lack of boundaries or difficulty setting boundaries in our adult lives and in our relationships. This is often the case in families where it wasn't safe to express feelings or emotions, families that are bonded through trauma, or in families where the parents were carrying their own wounds from the past and were unable to set clear parent–child boundaries.

In the same way your nervous-system ninjas jump in to protect you when they feel unsafe, your boundaries are your conscious way of protecting yourself. They're the foundation you can set for your own relationships as ensuring your relationships are built on solid foundations will mean they can stand the test of time. When your boundaries are in place, you'll feel seen, heard, respected and safe in your relationships, which in turn regulates your nervous system, leading to happier and healthier relationships.

Whose boundaries you're setting

An often-misunderstood element around setting boundaries in relationships is regarding you setting boundaries for the other person / your partner in the relationship; however, the only things you have control over are your own actions, and therefore boundaries are set for you, not your partner, because you're the only person who can decide if something is safe/unsafe or good/bad for you. So, the first lesson in setting boundaries is that you're to set them for yourself.

How to set your boundaries

To set your relationship boundaries, think about all the aspects of having a relationship – how to relate to each other, physical touch and health, emotional health and well-being, sex and finances – and what your preferences are. Don't forget that all relationships have ups and downs, so set boundaries around how you prefer to deal with and resolve disagreements.

Here are some lists of questions for you to think about:

- How do you relate to each other?
- What's okay and what's not okay for you in relationships?
- What makes you feel safe and what makes you feel unsafe in relationships?

- What values are most important to you?
- What's your preferred love language?
- What's your preferred way to communicate in relationships – phone, text, etc.?
- How often would you like to see your partner?
- How much time together and apart works for you in a relationship?
- What's a suitable timeframe for a partner to respond to a call or text?
- What are the deal-breakers for you in relationships?

Emotional boundaries

- How do you prefer to share your feelings with a partner?
- Do you share your feelings upfront or wait for something to happen before talking about your feelings?
- When you share your feelings, do you prefer a partner to listen or to jump in with a solution if you are feeling bad?
- What are your boundaries around criticising or judging within a relationship?

Physical health and touch

- What physical health activities do you currently have in place that are non-negotiables in your relationships (as an example, a regular yoga class or exercise class)?

- If physical health is a priority for you and health is one of your core values, what kind of physical health routine and attitude to it do you like to see in a partner?

- In terms of physical touch, do you prefer someone who's touchy feely, holding hands, etc., or do you prefer to keep physical touch for the bedroom? Think back to your preferred love language.

Sex

As we've discovered earlier, people with some attachment styles struggle with intimacy until they feel more secure in themselves and their relationships, so think about the following:

- What's a comfortable timeframe for you to begin a sexual relationship with a partner?

- What do you like and not like when it comes to sex?

- What are any complete deal-breakers for you when it comes to sex?

Finances

- What are your limits around financial boundaries?

- Do you prefer your partners to earn more than you or are you happy to be the main breadwinner?

Dealing with difficulties in relationships

When you face a difficulty in a relationship, how do you prefer to resolve it? [Please circle the one that resonates.]

- ♥ Take some time to regulate yourself and then discuss it

- ♥ Sleep on it

- ♥ Resolve it there and then, even if it's uncomfortable

- ♥ Never go to bed on an argument

- ♥ [Other]...

When setting boundaries, remember that you aren't giving your partner an ultimatum, you're simply communicating your needs and your boundaries. To a securely attached partner, this is a healthy conversation to have and one that they'll respect you for as they too will have boundaries they'd like to feel they can share with you.

Once you've considered the questions listed previously, I'd suggest making a master list of boundaries that you can communicate to your partners throughout the different stages of your relationships.

Communicating your boundaries

Your boundaries are yours to set. They're part of your new relationship blueprint and will help you to choose partners wisely, so if you're currently single and thinking about getting back into dating again, your boundaries should be discussed early on when you're finding out about your potential new partner. An easy way to discuss some of your boundaries is by having an open conversation around your potential partner's values and goals in life. Perhaps start by sharing your values and goals, and then see how aligned theirs are to yours.

You can also talk about attachment styles in relationships by telling them the following [finish the prompt]:

I feel secure in relationships when...

....

....

....

I feel anxious in relationships when...

....

....

....

I tend to sabotage relationships when...

....

....

....

I run from relationships when...

....

....

....

Then ask your partner to share how they feel and behave in relationships.

Setting boundaries is also an opportunity for you to assess what made you feel unsafe in previous relationships and what patterns you've seen in previous relationships that didn't work out; this will help you to become more consciously aware of them and set healthy boundaries going forward so history doesn't repeat itself.

An example of this would be setting boundaries around the following:

- When you see red flags, you'll take time to acknowledge them.
- When a potential partner is telling you he loves you in the first week after you met, you'll take time to acknowledge that this could be a warning sign.
- When a potential partner gaslights you, you'll acknowledge this as a warning sign.

You can also explain how you felt unsafe in previous relationships and then set boundaries around that.

When communicating your boundaries, there doesn't need to be an official meeting to do so; instead, just explain to your potential partner or current partner (if you're presently in a relationship) that you'd like to talk about what a healthy and happy relationship looks like to each of you, openly sharing and discussing boundaries without judgement. You can even make it a fun conversion by comparing boundaries, values and deal-breakers.

Maintaining your boundaries

Maintaining your boundaries is your job now. It's your way of showing yourself self-love and self-care, and it's your way of making yourself feel seen, heard and safe.

Once you've communicated your boundaries, it's so important that you stick to them. I know this can be hard, especially if you've been people-pleasing and putting others needs before your own, but this is now your time. It's your time to be there for yourself and to keep your inner child feeling safe, protected and cared for. By prioritising your own needs, you aren't being selfish – rather, you're giving yourself some self-love and honouring the beautiful, shiny diamond that sits within you. By sticking to your boundaries, you're sending yourself and your nervous system a message to say this:

I am enough.

I am lovable.

I am worthy.

And believe me, nobody can make you feel more loved, worthy and sufficient than you can, as your relationship with yourself is the only relationship that's ever guaranteed to last, it's the longest and most trustworthy relationship you'll ever have, it's the most loyal and lovable relationship you'll ever have, and it's the only one that has the power within it to protect, care for, nurture and love you.

> *"Daring to set boundaries is about having the courage to love ourselves, even when we risk disappointing others."*
> *– Brene Brown*

Will everyone like your new boundaries? The honest answer is no, but it's important to remember that the only people who'll be disappointed when you set boundaries are those who were benefitting from you having no boundaries. This can be a hard pill to swallow, especially if you've been people-pleasing and prioritising everyone else's needs over your own, but please remember this: all healthy relationships have boundaries, so to have healthy and happy relationships, boundaries are essential, and partners, family members or friends with a secure attachment style will not only completely get you setting boundaries but they'll respect and celebrate you for having the courage to be clear on what you want and what you will and won't accept. If you have children, you'll also be giving them the greatest gift of all as you'll be showing them that they matter and the importance of setting clear boundaries in their lives.

Self-discipline

Finally, we have self-discipline. Healing is a journey, not a destination, and it's self-discipline that keeps you on the journey and on the right track. Self-discipline is about giving yourself time to heal on your journey; it's about ensuring you stick to your boundaries, as in doing so, you're respecting yourself and your wishes; and it's about making certain that you show yourself kindness and compassion, and if you find yourself slipping back into old habits, you pull yourself back up again quickly.

A fellow positive-psychology coach shared a lesson with me that has not only stuck with me on my own journey but it has also really helped me to understand the importance of self-discipline. I hope it also helps you. The lesson is this:

"The highest form of self-love is self-discipline."
– Katrina Jones

This is self-discipline to love yourself first as it's only when you love yourself that you can truly identify love and give and receive love.

So you see, self-love is much more than just being nice to yourself: it's about being disciplined with yourself so you take the time to become more self-aware and accept all of you, just as you are; and it's about respecting yourself and your needs by setting healthy boundaries to let people know what you will and won't accept and how you like to be treated. And when those boundaries are respected and you've given yourself some self-love, your self-esteem and self-worth will increase as a result.

Learning to love yourself is by far the toughest part of this journey, but it's the greatest gift you'll ever give yourself, because if you don't have self-love, you can't truly love another as you can't give what you don't have, and without self-love, you risk settling for breadcrumbs of love as you won't know how to receive love.

Our greatest need of all is love: to love and to be loved. That journey starts with you loving yourself first so you can give and receive love. By reading this book, you're already starting on your self-love journey, so congratulations for taking the first step.

Before we look at what other steps you can take to continue your journey, let's have a look at your existing self-love score.

For each of the following, please rate your current level, giving yourself a score between 1 and 10, with 10 being excellent and 1 being not so good:

- Self-acceptance...........................
- Self-worth...................................
- Self-esteem.................................
- Self-care....................................
- Setting boundaries.....................
- Self-discipline.............................

Lastly, in the reflection exercise on the opposite page, think of some positive actions you can take for each of the six aspects of self-love so as to increase your score and love for yourself.

Reflection exercise

"To attract and maintain truly loving and happy relationships in your life, there are two things you must do.

"The first is to believe you're worthy and deserving of love, and the second is to let it in."

– Fiona Challis

CONCLUSION

Let's go back to the start of this book and the very first question we asked: what's wrong with me?

I hope you can now see there's nothing wrong with you; in fact, everything is right with you. For years, your subconscious mind, programming, protector parts and nervous system have been keeping you safe by holding you in the old familiar and by protecting you against perceived threats. The beautiful, innocent little girl within you learned quickly how to get love and connection and how to fit in and belong, and you survived together and made it through your childhood to be here today. However, the wounds from your past keep showing up in your relationships and life, not with the intention to hurt you but with the intention to show you what still needs to healed. By reading this book and investing time in yourself, you're telling your whole self that you're now ready to heal, to rewrite your story, to take over and reparent your inner child so as to give her the love she deserves, and to update your relationship blueprint through the lens of the informed adult you are today, so you can have secure, happy, healthy and loving relationships with yourself and others.

Let's bring everything together and look at your current relationship blueprint to identify the steps you can take to update it to a more secure relationship blueprint.

To complete your current (and soon to be previous) relationship blueprint, simply finish the following sentences (you've completed this previously in the book, but when you see your answers all together, everything will make sense):

The wounds I've identified that I was carrying from the past were...

....

....

....

The primary attachment style I formed growing up was...

....

The role I played growing up to fit in and belong was...

....

The beliefs I formed as a child were...

....

....

....

The parts of me that have been showing up in relationships were...

....

....

....

My inner child is activated in relationships when...

....

....

....

In stressful situations, I typically go into a **flight, fight, fawn** or **freeze** [circle the appropriate answer] stress response state.

When my system perceives a threat, my team of nervous-system ninjas typically take me to a **ventral vagal complex, sympathetic nervous system, dorsal ventral complex** or **freeze** [circle the appropriate answer] state.

The trauma and wounds from my past show up in my body... [where] and the way they show up is... [how].

....

....

....

Looking back on your relationships, how secure have you felt?

....

What was your self-love score (from 1-10):

....

When you look at your relationship blueprint in black and white, I hope you can now begin to see that it's completely understandable why you've been experiencing the same destructive patterns in relationships. I hope you can begin to show yourself some self-compassion and self-love, as this relationship blueprint didn't start with you, and most of it was formed through the eyes of a beautiful, innocent young girl who was just seeking her birthright of having true love and connection. Your current relationship blueprint isn't your fault, but it is your responsibility to change.

Before we bring all nine steps together, please take a moment to reflect on at least five positive actions you can take as a result of reading this book that will enable you to rewrite your relationship blueprint so you can attract and maintain healthy, happy and loving relationships in your life.

The positive actions I will take are these:

1. ....

2. ....

3. ....

4. ....

5. ....

Now let's bring together all nine steps of change that we've looked at throughout this book, which are the exact same nine steps I took on my own 'eat, pray, self-love' journey.

Step 1 – Heal your past wounds

Heal yourself from the wounds of your past. Until I started this journey, I was oblivious to my abandonment wounds and other wounds I'd been carrying from the trauma of my dysfunctional childhood. Once I was able to identify these wounds, I could feel them and then heal them, and in doing so, I was able to let go of a ton of baggage that I felt had been weighing me down for years. This is a critical first step, as without identifying and healing these wounds, we carry them with us from one relationship to the next. I like to think of these wounds as bags on an airport baggage carousel, which keep going round and round until you pick up the bag and then feel it to heal it.

Step 2 – Attachment styles

Understand your attachment style, which is who you show up as in relationships. It's why you may experience fears of rejection or abandonment, why you might sabotage relationships, or why you avoid relationships completely. By understanding your attachment style, you can take steps to become more securely attached, and you can share your attachment style in relationships so you can both make each other feel more secure. You can also begin to identify the attachment style of your partner or potential partner, so you can see early on if you're compatible with each other or what adjustments you could implement to make your relationship healthier and happier.

Step 3 – Programming & patterns

Over the years, we've all formed beliefs, those beliefs then shape your thoughts, and your thoughts then dictate your actions and behaviours in relationships. These beliefs and thoughts happen subconsciously, and you'll have become programmed by them, meaning they show up in your relationships automatically, but the program needs to be updated as it's running on a set of outdated beliefs. In this step, you reset the program by turning your limiting and disempowering beliefs into more empowering and loving beliefs.

Step 4 – Protector parts

Remember the story of the golden Buddha that was hidden beneath a layer of clay? (Relayed in *Step 5*.) Your beliefs, thoughts and patterns form that layer of clay in your relationships. It becomes a part of you that shows up to protect you, like the most loyal employee ever, but this part has been formed based on outdated beliefs that are now preventing you from being your authentic self in relationships. Therefore, *Step 4* is asking that part of you to go by showing it you're now safe or giving it an alternative role so it helps you, not hinders you, in relationships.

Step 5 – Inner child

We all have an inner child within us who just wants to be loved and who wants to feel seen, heard and acknowledged. When she doesn't, we're activated, as it brings us right back to being a young girl in a time, place or scene when we didn't feel loved, or to when it was perhaps unsafe to be heard or scary to be seen. Growing up, we may not have had the love and connection we needed from our caregivers, but that was in the past. In the present, it's your role to be the loving parent your inner child needs, and it's never too late to give her the childhood she didn't have. This is your time to reparent, to love and to cherish your inner child, as when she feels loved, safe and happy, you can feel safe, loved and happy in your relationships.

Step 6 – Nervous system regulation

For me, *Step 6* was the missing link. I'd done so much work on myself up until this stage; I'd been to therapy, attended every seminar and masterclass I could, read hundreds of books and listened to tons of podcasts, but I still felt stuck until I discovered I needed to show, not tell, my team of nervous-system ninjas that I was safe. Understanding how my autonomic nervous system works was a true light bulb moment for me as it helped me to understand why I had very few memories from my childhood and why I dissociated and disconnected so much. Understanding how your system works and showing it that it's safe to take small steps of change is the key to helping you get yourself unstuck.

Step 7 – Embodied & somatic healing

During the previous steps, I'd learned so much incredible information about myself and felt I was healing on both a conscious and subconscious level, but in *Step 7*, I sensed I was healing all of me as this was when I learned how to take an embodied healing approach. This approach taught me how to integrate the physical, mental, emotional and spiritual aspects of my healing and how to take the first crucial step of regulating my nervous system, which is the key to creating long and lasting change. By taking an embodied approach to your healing, you can finally be free from the chains of the past that have kept you from being your whole and authentic self in relationships.

Step 8 – Secure self

Once I'd completed the previous steps, I finally felt ready to step into my future self; however, after years of showing up in relationships as a wounded version of myself, I discovered that I barely knew who I was, what I wanted and how I wanted to be loved. In this step, I felt like I was allowing my old self to leave and a new best version of myself to emerge; I loved getting to know and understand myself, my values and my love language more. By letting the old version of yourself go in this step, you make way for a beautiful, new you to emerge when you know what you want, what you value and how you like to be loved. This is a truly empowering step that will leave you feeling so excited about your future.

Step 9 – Self-love

In the last stage of my journey, my true transformation happened, as for the first time in my life, I learned how to love myself. I was able to seek the love and connection I needed internally rather than externally. I was finally able to see who I was, what I wanted, what was important to me, how I wanted to be loved, and what I would and wouldn't accept in relationships. It took 48 years for me to realise this, but when I did, I felt so alive again, as if I'd finally come home to me again and I was stepping into a new lease of life. I broke free from the chains of the past, let go of anything holding me back and I accepted all of me, even the flaws.

I began to understand that true self-love is much more than a woo-woo phrase and having lovely bubble baths and treats. It's about having self-awareness, self-acceptance and healthy self-care practices; working on my self-worth and self-esteem; setting boundaries; and having the self-discipline to stick to my practices and boundaries and to honour myself and my needs.

For my entire life up until that point, I believed I needed to be in a romantic relationship to feel loved; I believed I needed to be liked by everyone to be loved; I believed everyone else's needs were more important than mine; and I believed I had to be the good girl, the fixer and the overachiever to get love. However, it wasn't until this step that I could see just how much I'd abandoned myself to get love from others. That in itself is ironic, as in relationships, one of my greatest fears was being abandoned, yet here I was, abandoning myself.

Our greatest need of all is love – to both love and be loved – but that greatest love is already within all of us. That loving and lifelong relationship we seek is already within us – we just need to learn how to access it. Learning to love yourself is the greatest gift you can ever give yourself, as when you learn how to love yourself, you can then give love to others and receive love from others.

The happy ending

I wrote this book and created **The H.A.P.P.I.N.E.S.S Code**™ as I wanted to provide women just like me with a step-by-step guide that would take them on a similar journey of self-discovery so they too could rewrite their stories, heal, be happy, and get the love that they deserve from themselves and within relationships.

I hope the steps you've taken within this book have carried you on a similar journey and you can now start to emerge as the new, more secure you, with a new relationship blueprint, and renewed senses of self-worth, self-esteem and self-love. However, I hope the journey doesn't end here, as this book finishes. Instead, I hope you'll stay on this journey of having self-love, as when you do, true authentic love and happiness come to you.

> *"I'm not afraid of storms, for I am learning how to sail my ship." – Louisa May Alcott*

Before we end this journey together, I'd love to leave you with a beautiful positive-psychology metaphor that I share with all my clients, called 'the sailing ship metaphor'; it's a fantastic way to help you understand just how powerful the inner work you've just completed is and how it will help you to navigate your way successfully within relation**ships**. As let's be honest, even with the best therapy and coaching in the world, and even in the most secure relationships, relationships aren't always plain sailing, and at times, they'll hit rocky patches. However, it's not about the rocky patches; it's about how you weather the storm and the tools you have to make it to your destination.

The sailing ship metaphor

In the sailing ship metaphor, see yourself as the ship. For a ship to sail smoothly and stay on course, there are certain elements that need to be in place to make it through any rocky patches, just like in relationships. Knowing what you now know from the steps you've taken within this book, you can influence these elements to work with you rather than against you, which will mean you get to your destination faster.

Destination (best-possible self and relationship with self)

Think about the 'your best-possible self' exercise we did in *Step 8*. What did the best-possible you look like, feel like and have? What defined your best-possible relationships? This is the destination you're heading for. For some of you, that destination may be to have a healthy, happy and loving relationship in which you feel valued, respected and cherished, but for others, it may be to have a more secure relationship with yourself first so you can work on increasing your self-worth, self-esteem and self-love. There's no right or wrong, as the destination is your choice but remember the most important relationship you have is the one you have with yourself as that shapes all other relationships in your life.

The anchor (your past and your old programming)

If you let the anchor down, you'll stay stuck, as a ship can't move forwards when it's anchored. So, to begin your journey, you must raise your anchor and let go of your past. If you feel stuck at times on your journey, simply check in with yourself and ask yourself if your anchor is up or down and if you're operating on old beliefs, patterns and programming.

Water (your environment)

Every boat needs water to move on, but be careful of the water that's surrounding your boat, as some of it will help you move forwards easily, but other parts of it could cause you to remain stuck in stormy waters.

When you're healing and want to move forwards in your life and your relationships, the environment you place yourself in is going to be incredibly important. As an example, if you've had the unfortunate experience of being in a narcissistic relationship and you want to heal, move on and become more secure yourself, then being in lots of Facebook groups that are constantly comparing narcissistic experiences isn't going to help you move forwards; it will only keep you stuck.

Hurt people hurt people; healed people heal people.

If you want to heal and be happy, place yourself in environments where you can be around more women who're healed and happy.

Compass (your values)

Your values that we identified in *Step 8* are what make you feel aligned; they're like your internal compass, which helps to keep you on the right path and identify when you're steering off it. Your values guide how you think, feel and behave, and they give your life meaning and purpose.

If you hit any rocky patches on your journey or something doesn't feel right, just come back to your values and ask yourself whether what's happening is aligned to your values or not, and that will give you your answer.

Steering wheel (your nervous system)

Your team of nervous-system ninjas will always be steering your ship. Remember that your loyal security guard (neuroception) is going to do its googling equivalent to see if any situations you come up against on your journey are safe, dangerous or life-threatening. If you want to go in a new direction, but your nervous system doesn't have any saved experiences to show it that it's safe, it will do its job to keep you safe, so remember that, to move forwards and to have new experiences on your journey, you must show, not tell, your system that it's safe. When it feel safes, it will work with you.

Weather (external circumstances)

Sometimes, the wind is blowing in our sails, and we can easily sail towards our destination. At other times, the wind and the rain make it difficult to keep travelling in our preferred direction.

On your way, you'll no doubt encounter some external circumstances that you have no control over. This could be family, work, being around negative people or sickness to name but a few. The key to navigating your way through the weather successfully is focusing your efforts on what you can control, not what you can't control. Things you can control include your emotions, self-talk (that is, the words you're saying and the pictures you're painting in your mind), thoughts and behaviours, so focus on them in your journey ahead.

Leaks (lack of boundaries)

Just like leaks are considered 'internal' problems for a ship, a lack of boundaries in relationships can be considered an internal problem. Putting boundaries in place is an act of self-love, and in secure relationships, they're healthy and to be respected. So, to secure any leaks in your ship, set and stick to your boundaries, as they're yours to make and yours to keep. By allowing people to disrespect your boundaries, you're allowing leaks in your ship, which will impact your journey over time.

Sails (self-love)

Without the ship's sails, it would float aimlessly in the water, not going anywhere. This is just like how, without self-love, relationships can float aimlessly and go nowhere. Having self-love allows you to flourish in relationships. Your sails will allow your ship to move in the right direction, to generate momentum and to help you (the captain) to create a journey that's worth travelling. A woman who has self-love in relationships can open her heart to give and receive true love, so open your sails, ladies, and in doing so, you'll sail at full speed ahead with the wind in your sails.

Other ships (your relationship with others)

I have intentionally placed the 'Other ships' section after 'Sails', as 'Other ships' represents the relationships you have with others. This can include romantic relationships or relationships with your family, friends or colleagues. Although we are relational beings and need other relationships in our lives to meet our needs for belonging and connection, the most important relationship you'll ever have in your life is the relationship you have with yourself.

When you have a secure relationship with yourself, you can choose what other ships you want to have with you on your journey. Other ships can influence you in many ways, both positively and negatively. For instance, when you decide to turn the steering wheel and take a different course, you may experience support from people who motivate you to pursue your new direction. At the same time, others may disapprove of the new direction and provoke feelings of self-doubt and fear within you.

But when you have that secure relationship with yourself, you'll be able to keep yourself on the right track on your journey, and you won't allow other ships to take you off course.

The captain (you)

Last but by no means least, every sailing ship needs a captain, and that captain is you. The captain decides where the boat is going, plans the route to get there, navigates the way through any stormy waters and keeps it on track until it arrives at its destination.

By reading this book, you're becoming the captain of your own ship. You've chosen your destination. You have a step-by-step plan to get there and the tools needed to navigate any stormy waters. Doing all the inner work in this book will keep you on track, as you'll be showing yourself at the mental, emotional, physical and spiritual levels that it's now safe to heal, get unstuck, open your sails, open your heart and let love in again. Only two things remain for you to do once our journey together ends. First, take radical responsibility for implementing the steps within this book so it's not just another book you've read but it's the book that's given you the building blocks you need to break free from your past and to build a solid foundation for healthy, happy and loving relationships. Second, believe you're worthy and deserving of love, so remind yourself of the following daily:

You are worthy.

You are enough.

You are lovable.

And you are, my dear! You are worthy and deserving of true love and happiness so keep showing up for yourself by staying on this journey and sticking to your 'commit don't quit promise' that you made at the start of this book as by continuing to do this work you will be *profoundly impacting* your own life and relationships and of those around you.

For my final words in our time together, I'm going to leave you with the only words that have stuck with me after years of being dragged to Catholic church every Sunday as a child. As the service ended, we'd shake hands with our fellow churchgoers as we left, saying

Peace be with you.

WHAT'S NEXT

How to stay on your journey

Ladies, first, I want to take a moment to acknowledge you for showing up for yourself and doing the inner work in this book. By doing so, you're showing and telling every part of you that you're worth it, you're enough, and you do deserve true love and happiness – and you do! Within this book, you've shone a light on your past; you've chipped through the clay so you can now become more present and shine as the true, authentic you; and you now have a new relationship blueprint that will help you to have secure, healthy, happy and truly loving relationships with yourself and others in the future. So, from the bottom of my heart, congratulations! I'm so proud of you and feel truly honoured that you've trusted me to be your guide on this truly transformational journey.

Your next steps are to continue saying yes to yourself, to continue showing up for yourself and to continue investing time in yourself.

For some of you reading this book, you'll have got everything you needed within this book and prefer to continue your journey alone. For others of you, you may wish to continue to work with me, either on a one-to-one basis or within my The H.A.P.P.I.N.E.S.S Code™

group program, so you can be heard, heal and be happy within an environment of bad-ass women who are all saying yes to themselves and are no longer willing to settle for anything less than true love and happiness – which is contagious. Both are fantastic ways to self-regulate and co-regulate your nervous system and to show your system that healing and happiness are safe and available to you.

If you're ready to take this journey a step further and work together with me to create your happiest life and relationship yet, then check out my website or follow me on social media (links are as follows) where I can continue to support you on your journey.

Connect with me here:

Website – www.rapidrelationshiptherapy.com

Facebook – @FionaChallisCoaching

Instagram – @rapidrelationshiptherapy

Until then, I'm sending you lots of love, and again, congratulations to you!

Fi xx

Scan me for instant access

REFERENCES

1. Gilbert, E. (2007). *Eat pray love: One woman's search for everything.* London: Bloomsbury Paperbacks.

2. Gardner, D. (producer) and Murphy, R. (director) (2010). *Eat pray love* [Film]. Columbia Pictures; Plan B Entertainment.

3. Holmes, J. (2014). *John Bowlby and attachment theory.* Abingdon: Routledge.

4. Levine, A. and Heller, R.S.F. (2019). *Attached: Are you anxious, avoidant or secure? How the science of adult attachment can help you find – and keep – love.* Monument, CO: Bluebird.

5. Hazan, C. and Shaver, P. (1987). Romantic love conceptualized as an attachment process. *Journal of Personality and Social Psychology, 52*(3), 511–524. https://doi.org/10.1037/0022-3514.52.3.511

6. Rosenburg, R. (2013). *The human magnet syndrome: Why we love people who hurt us.* s.l.: Premier Publishing & Media.

7. Rosenburg, R. (2013). *The human magnet syndrome: Why we love people who hurt us.* s.l.: Premier Publishing & Media.

8. Rosenburg, R. (2013). *The human magnet syndrome: Why we love people who hurt us.* s.l.: Premier Publishing & Media.

9. Levine, A. and Heller, R.S.F. (2019). *Attached: Are you anxious, avoidant or secure? How the science of adult attachment can help you find – and keep – love.* Monument, CO: Bluebird.

10. Perel, E. (2017). *Mating in captivity: Unlocking erotic intelligence.* New York, NY: Harper Paperbacks.

11. Porges, S. (n.d.). *Stephen W. Porges polyvagal theory.* [Online] Available at: https://www.stephenporges.com/

12. Le Pera, N. (2018). *How to know if your gut is healthy.* [Online] Available at: https://theholisticpsychologist.com/how-to-know-if-your-gut-is-healthy/

13. Maté, G. (n.d.). *Mind/body health.* [Online] Available at: https://drgabormate.com/mindbody-health/

14. Van Der Kolk, B. (2015). *The body keeps the score: Brain, mind, and body in the healing of trauma.* London: Penguin.

15. Le Pera, N. (2018). *How to know if your gut is healthy.* [Online] Available at: https://theholisticpsychologist.com/how-to-know-if-your-gut-is-healthy/

16. Jampolsky, G. (2021). *Oprah explains how forgiveness can change the way you move through the world.* Oprah Daily. [Online] Available at: https://www.oprahdaily.com/life/a37117486/oprah-forgiveness/

17. Jampolsky, G. (2021). *Oprah explains how forgiveness can change the way you move through the world.* Oprah Daily. [Online] Available at: https://www.oprahdaily.com/life/a37117486/oprah-forgiveness/

18. VIA (n.d.). *Character strengths and virtues: A handbook and classification.* [Online] Available at: https://www.viacharacter.org/character-strengths-and-virtues

19. Chapman, G. (2015). *The 5 love languages: The secret to love that lasts.* Chicago, IL: Moody Publishers.

20. Robinson, L., Segal, J., and Smith, M. (2022). *The mental health benefits of exercise.* HelpGuide. [Online] Available at: https://www.helpguide.org/articles/healthy-living/the-mental-health-benefits-of-exercise.htm

21. Robinson, L., Segal, J., and Smith, M. (2022). *The mental health benefits of exercise.* HelpGuide. [Online] Available at: https://www.helpguide.org/articles/healthy-living/the-mental-health-benefits-of-exercise.htm

22. Scott, E. (2022). *The toxic effects of negative self-talk.* Verywellmind. [Online] Available at: https://www.verywellmind.com/negative-self-talk-and-how-it-affects-us-4161304

23. Millacci, T.S. (2017). *What is gratitude and why is it so important?* Positive Psychology. [Online] Available at: https://positivepsychology.com/gratitude-appreciation/

24. Howes, L. (n.d.). *School of greatness.* [Podcast series] Available at: https://lewishowes.com/sogpodcast/

25. Maté, G. (2019). *When the body says no: The cost of hidden stress.* London: Vermilion.

ADDITIONAL RECOMMENDED READING

Anderson, S. (2014). *The journey from abandonment to healing*. London: Berkeley Publishing Group.

Beattie, M. (2018). *Beyond co-dependency*. Center City, MN: Hazelden Publishing.

Cole, T. (2021). *Boundary boss: The essential guide to talk true, be seen, and (finally) live free*. Louisville, CO: Sounds True Inc.

Dyer, W. (2007). *Change your thoughts, change your life: Living the wisdom of the Tao*. London: Hay House UK.

Le Pera, N. (2021). *How to do the work*. London: Orion Spring.

Levine, A. and Heller, R.S.F. (2019). *Attached: Are you anxious, avoidant or secure? How the science of adult attachment can help you find – and keep – love*. Monument, CO: Bluebird.

Levine, P.A. (1997). *Waking the tiger: Healing trauma*. Berkely, CA: North Atlantic Books, US.

Maté, G. and Maté, D. (2022). *The myth of normal: Trauma, illness & healing in a toxic culture*. London: Vermilion.

Perry, P. (2020). *The book your wish your parents had read (and your children will be glad that you did)*. London: Penguin Life.

Porges, S. (2017). *The pocket guide to polyvagal theory: The transformative power of feeling safe.* New York, NY: W.W. Norton & Company.

Rosenburg, R. (2013). *The human magnet syndrome: Why we love people who hurt us.* s.l.: Premier Publishing & Media.

Singer, M.A. (2007). *The untethered soul.* Oakland, CA: New Harbinger Publications, US.

Strawson, C. (2022). *The unseen wounds of women.* s.l.: Caroline Strawson Global Enterprises Ltd.

Tolle, E. (2009). *A new earth.* London: Penguin.

Van Der Kolk, B. (2015). *The body keeps the score: Brain, mind, and body in the healing of trauma.* London: Penguin.

Wolynn, M. (2022). *It didn't start with you.* London: Vermilion.

ACKNOWLEDGEMENTS

Both my own healing and this book would never have happened without some very special people whom I'm eternally grateful for coming into my life and joining me on what has been a truly amazing, liberating and transformational journey of healing and self-discovery.

First, I want to acknowledge every single woman I've ever worked with and every woman who picks up this book. By doing so, you're saying you're ready to heal, to let go, and to have the love and happiness you deserve. Your courage to do the inner work on this journey, your trust in me to guide you, and the impact that your healing will have on future generations is what inspired me to write this book and what motivates me daily.

I'd like to thank every therapist, coach and mentor I was blessed to meet on my own healing journey. In particular, I'd like to acknowledge Marissa Peer, who's the founder of Rapid Transformational Therapy® (RTT), and my wonderful family of RTT therapists. You helped me through the darkest time, and with this truly amazing therapy and your support, I was finally able to understand and let go of my past, and then let the light and love back in again.

I'd also like to thank Niyc Pidgeon, Mel Deague and my fellow positive-psychology coaches. You've helped me create and follow my path towards true happiness, and to create the powerful, purposeful and meaningful changes I needed to make to live the fulfilled life I'm incredibly grateful to live today.

A huge thank you to Stephen Porges, founder of polyvagal theory; Nicole Le Pera, the Holistic Psychologist, and Caroline Strawson, founder of Narcissistic Trauma Unlocking, trauma-informed positive-psychology coach and somatic therapist. Together, your research and teachings on nervous-system regulation and somatic healing have helped me find the missing piece of my healing puzzle, which I'll always be eternally grateful for.

A special shout out to Andy Harrington, founder of The Professional Speakers Academy; and Niyc Pidgeon, founder of Unstoppable Success. You've always believed in me and have both been instrumental in helping me to deliver the teachings and life lessons within this book and in supporting me to reach my mission of transforming the lives of 1 million women and children.

I'd also like to give my gratitude to my team for helping me to pull this book together and for keeping me sane along the journey by taking over all the technical and publishing support I needed.

Thank you to my wonderful friends – I'm truly blessed to have you in my life. You picked me up, dusted me off and helped me start all over again, without judgement, when my relationships didn't work out, and that will always mean the world to me. A special thanks to Gaynor, Philly, Tracy, Denise, Sheri and Aminah. You mean the world to me, and I love you all dearly.

Finally, I would love to acknowledge and thank my family.

My son Jamie. Being your mother will always be the greatest honour of my life, and I truly treasure the love we'll always have.

My siblings, who were my rocks growing up; to my parents (especially my mother who single handedly raised seven children), my grandparents and every generation before them who all did the very best they could, despite all having had incredibly difficult childhoods and living in a time where therapy and coaching weren't readily available to help them heal and let go of their own trauma. The unresolved trauma that has been in our family for many generations has served as a catalyst for me to resolve my own trauma, and in doing so together, we're breaking the cycle for this generation and the future generations in our family.

Lastly I'd like to thank, every man who ever hurt me and every relationship that didn't work out. You have been my greatest teachers of all, as you've unintentionally showed me everything I still needed to heal, and that has given me the gift of now living a life with purpose and meaning and the gift of finding true love and happiness.

ABOUT THE AUTHOR

Fiona Challis is a licensed Rapid Transformational Therapy®️ therapist, licensed hypnotherapist, positive-psychology coach, trauma-informed and somatic-healing coach, life coach, neuro-linguistic programming (NLP) practitioner, and founder of **The H.A.P.P.I.N.E.S.S Code™️**.

Her mission is to transform the lives of 1 million women who, like her, seem to have the knack of attracting the wrong partners and see the same destructive patterns show up in their relationships. She'll do this by helping them to break free from their past and rewrite their stories and relationship blueprints, so they can have both the true love and happiness they deserve and secure and healthy relationships.

Fiona is passionate about helping families to break generational patterns. Her one-to-one and group therapy and coaching programs enable the women she supports to break their vicious cycles, as through healing themselves, they have a profound impact and ripple effect on their entire family and future generations. Fiona also plans to bring her teachings and **The H.A.P.P.I.N.E.S.S Code™** into schools in the near future with the aim of children learning much earlier in life how to have happiness within themselves and the importance of putting self-love first, so they can go on to have secure, healthy, happy and loving relationships in the future.

Clients who've worked with Fiona have said her work is truly transformational, she provides a safe and empathic space to help her clients heal without spending years in therapy, and her enthusiasm and happiness are contagious.

She's originally from a small town called Enniskillen in Northern Ireland and currently lives in Pangbourne in England. She's one of seven children and a devoted mother to her son, Jamie.